The Written and the Spoken.

Literacy and oral transmission among the Uyghur

Ildikó Bellér-Hann

Contents

Introduction
The region and the people..1
The topic 3
The sources..7

Chapter I: The written word before 1949
1 Economic transaction 10
2 Dispute settlements..14
3 Marriage and divorce..15
4 Private communication 16
5 Popular practices 17
6 Literacy and beliefs 19
Summary...29

Chapter II: Oral solutions and the interface between oral and written transmission
1 The oral option 30
2 The mixing of modes 32
3 Performers 37
Summary...41

Chapter III: Education
1 *Mäktäp*..42
2 *Mädräsä*..49
3 The beginnings of modern education 56
Summary...66

Chapter IV: Literacy and oral transmission after 1949
1 Literacy and education..68
2 The persistence of oral transmission...73
3 Writing in the public sphere..81
4 Rumour...83
Summary...87

Conclusion 88

References 91

Introduction

The region and the people

This paper discusses aspects of literacy and oral transmission among the Uyghur in north-west China from the late nineteenth century up to the present day. The territory known previously as Eastern or Chinese Turkestan, and since 1955 as the Xinjiang Uyghur Autonomous Region (XUAR), is situated in the north-western corner of the People's Republic of China.[1] The region makes up about one-sixth of the country's total area. Despite its size and great strategic importance as a border area, its population is relatively small, at around seventeen million.[2] This vast border region has had a long history of Chinese presence going back to the Han dynasty (206.B.C. to 220. A.D). However, for a long time the Chinese were unable to establish firm control here. The region was incorporated into the Qing empire in the second half of the eighteenth century. Following the great Muslim rebellions of the nineteenth century it became an imperial province in 1884 when it was given its present name Xinjiang, meaning New Frontier. During the Republican period (1911-1949), although nominally part of China, control from the centre was again ineffective. The latest political incorporation of the region into China came with the communist victory of 1949. Modernisation has gained momentum in the socialist period, but the region has developed as an internal colony and shows many continuities with its pre-modern past.[3] Above all, local society has preserved its primarily agricultural character. Many rural families with ready access to markets engage in

---

1. For a general introduction to the region see for example Weggel 1984, Grobe-Hagel 1991. on issues of ethnicity see Rudelson 1997, Hoppe 1998.
2. Sautman 1998: 87.
3. Cf. Gladney 1998.

'sideline production' and derive their income from crafts and other, non-agricultural sources, but the overwhelming majority of the rural population continue to identify themselves as peasants.[4]

Today the People's Republic recognises fifty-five ethnic groups as minority nationals, of which ten are Muslim. The highest concentration of Muslims is found in the XUAR. Of the thirteen officially recognised ethnic groups living there, the dominant group is the Uyghur. They constitute the second largest Muslim group in China and the nominal majority in Xinjiang, numbering over seven million in 1990.[5] The Uyghur speak a Turkic language and their linguistic and religious affiliation form the basis of their ethnic identity. Their ethnogenesis was a complicated and complex process. Indigenous populations who spoke Indo-European languages, incoming Turkic speakers (among them the so-called Old Uyghur), Mongolian, Tibetan and other groups all contributed. The region experienced numerous religious traditions before conversion to Islam, which started around the tenth century and was more or less completed by the sixteenth century. Parallel to gradual Islamisation the region also experienced Turkicisation of the language and the switch to a sedentary lifestyle by incoming nomads. State recognition of the Muslims and later of the Uyghur as a distinct group was the decisive step in the emergence of the modern Uyghur. The ethnonym was revived only in the early twentieth century by Turkic speakers living outside the borders of China, and it attained wide currency among the local population only from the 1930s. Since most sources from before 1949 refer to the local population as *Turki*, I shall also use this ethnonym for the period prior to 1949, while *Uyghur* will be used for the modern period after this date.

In the discussion 1949, the communist occupation of the region represents the most important watershed, since it also

---

4. Bellér-Hann, I. 1997, 1998a, 1998b.
5. Mackerras 1998: 29.

marks the beginnings of accelerated social engineering and modernisation. A substantial part of the paper deals with pre-1949 materials. The term 'traditional' is used to refer to concepts and ideas rooted in local society before this date. 'Modern' is used to refer to the era introduced by the Chinese communist government after 1949. This simple periodisation, justified in terms of the main indices of social and economic development, corresponds also to the categories used not only by local bureaucrats but by ordinary people as well.

The topic

The study of verbal expressions of emotions, ideas and actions has been taken up by specialists in a number of disciplines over recent decades. Often the discussion has taken a dichotomous approach, problematising the apparently contrasting forms of literary and oral communication. Alongside specific case studies, scholars have sought theoretical generalisations concerning literacy and orality, and the complicated correlation between dominant modes of transmission and social and cultural processes.[6] Increasingly it has been shown that the old dichotomy of oral and written as monolithic and mutually exclusive is untenable.[7] It remains useful only as long as these categories are recognised as highly dynamic and variable in their social and spatial distribution and embeddedness. Prior to the advent of mass literacy, many societies in which the overwhelming majority of the population was non-literate were exposed to some

---

6. Finnegan 1977, 1988, 1992; Goody 1968, 1977, 1982, 1986, 1987; Heath 1983; Ong 1982. Street 1984, (ed.) 1993; Tonkin 1992; Vansina 1965, 1985.
7. For example, Finnegan calls the idea of a pure, 'uncontaminated' oral culture a myth (1977: 24), while Tonkin emphasises that orality and literacy cannot be easily distinguished. (1992: 14). Recent discussions in Islamic Studies concerning the transmission of traditions in the first centuries of Islam have also argued for a very early convergence of various forms of oral and written transmissions (e.g. Schoeler 1985, 1989, 1996).

degree of literacy.⁸ Some authors argue that, because literacy is such a highly variable and complex phenomenon, 'an investigation of this variety must take priority over the search for a priori, universalist generalisations.'⁹

Literacy and orality are essentially conceptualised here as social phenomena which are closely interconnected. They are broad, ideal types, each comprising a multitude of practices, a set of resources people can call upon according to need.¹⁰ This discussion is based on the premise that literacy is not the exclusive property of the élite, since all segments of local society had direct or indirect contact with the written word even prior to the emergence of modern mass education. I wish to problematise literacy and oral transmission within the context of popular culture, recognising the ordinary and commonplace as a 'legitimate object of inquiry'.¹¹ While the discussion necessarily includes references to people with specialised knowledge, it pays particular attention to the exposure of other, non-privileged segments of local society to the power of the written word. This seems appropriate in a society which has preserved its primarily peasant character down to the present day.¹²

It will be argued that, regardless of actual literacy skills, Islamic literate tradition played an important role in daily life for many people in Eastern Turkestan.¹³ The region had a long

---

8. Finnegan 1977: 23.
9. Street and Besnier 1994: 527.
10. Street and Besnier 1994.
11. Mukerji and Schudson 1991: 2.
12. The achievements of the Uyghur *literati* in modern times remain outside the scope of this paper. (See Rudelson 1997; Friederich 1997).
13. Islam did not, however, entail the exclusive dominance of the Arabic script. Foreign occupiers in the seventeenth and eighteenth centuries brought other scripts along and the presence of foreign merchants in the big market centres added further to the variety. This was continued in the twentieth century by Chinese and Russian economic and political rivalry. The situation was further complicated by the replacement of the Arabic script with a modified Latin alphabet in the 1960s among the Muslim minorities in the province. This was reversed in the early 1980s, and at present the Arabic script is in use. Nevertheless, people remain exposed to

history of literacy and a variety of scripts before the advent of Islam. Conversion to Islam among the oasis dwellers was more or less completed by the sixteenth century, and, as a 'religion of the Book', Islam introduced a new literate tradition and the Arabic script. Although a large section of the population must have been non-literate,[14] especially in rural areas, most people in all social groups had some awareness of the written word. Knowledge *about* though not necessarily knowledge *of* the written word influenced the mental worlds of men and women in virtually all social and occupational groups. The main areas of life where commoners were exposed to literacy were economic transactions, law, dealings with the supernatural, and education.[15] As we shall see, the borderlines between these areas were often blurred: economic transactions (including inheritance cases and donations to pious foundations), dispute settlements, marriage and divorce could all potentially end up in the Islamic courts. Both the operation of these courts and the organisation of education were intricately linked to mainstream religion, the former to codified forms of Islamic notions of justice, the latter to established *mäktäp* patterns, based on the study of religious texts. Although various forms of dealing with the supernatural often contradicted orthodox assumptions, these were most likely conceived by practitioners as being thoroughly Islamic.

The discussion concentrates on the Uyghur but two caveats must be entered at the outset. First, there is no attempt at an exhaustive discussion of the topic across the entire vast region where the Uyghur live. Rather, coverage is limited by the nature of the sources, which are discussed below. Second, I do not wish to reduce the oral and literate traditions of pre-

---

Chinese characters, while some oasis centres display Russian and English inscriptions for the benefit of tourists and businessmen.

14. In using the term 'non-literate' I follow Goody, who argues that in traditional settings lack of literate knowledge was not shameful and did not carry the same social stigma as being illiterate in modern western societies. (Goody 1987: 127).

15. In this classification I follow Goody (1987). References to traditional education will be further discussed in Chapter III below.

1949 Xinjiang to a Chinese - Uyghur dichotomy. In addition to these groups, many of the market centres had substantial communities of foreigners. Islamic learning continued to cultivate a degree of Persian and Arabic literate tradition, while the arrival of White Russians and the inclusion of large parts of the region into the economic interest sphere of the Soviet Union during the first half of the twentieth century must have spread awareness and knowledge of the Cyrillic script and the Russian language among some segments of the urban population. Although Western, especially Swedish, missionary activities made use of local (primarily Uyghur and Chinese) literate traditions, their very presence introduced still other traditions.

In his history of Muslims in Northwest China, Jonathan Lipman points out the types of accommodations reached by Chinese Muslims in the fields of language and literacy. As a result of reforms introduced in the sixteenth century, the shallowness of Arabic and Persian knowledge in the Islamic schools was mitigated by the introduction of Chinese phonetic pronunciation of Arabic. The Arabic orthography of the holy texts and the basic Islamic curriculum were retained. Since most people had not even basic literate knowledge of Chinese, this innovation had only limited impact. College (*mädräsä*)-educated Chinese Muslims during the late Ming period could speak Chinese but not read or write it, and they could read Arabic and Persian but not speak it. This asymmetrical linguistic situation led to the introduction of an Arabic transliteration system for Chinese characters. Lipman claims that this Arabic pinyin for Chinese 'remains extant among Chinese Muslims, though only a few use it regularly.'[16] We cannot be sure to what extent this practice among the Chinese Muslims of Xinjiang has persisted, but we may safely assume that the Uyghur of Xinjiang did *not* develop a comparable asymmetry. In the late nineteenth century Uyghur literate culture was thoroughly Islamic while the spoken language was never seriously threatened by Chinese. Local officials and

---

16. Lipman 1997: 50-1.

interpreters exercised direct social control over the rural and urban population with the aid of an Arabic script tradition that was closely associated with Islam. Chinese literate tradition played little or no role in the daily life of the population, the sole exceptions being the local administrators (*bäg*) and the interpreters who mediated between the Chinese overlords and the Turki/Uyghur taxpayers.[17] Nevertheless, there was a degree of direct contact between the local population and Chinese settlers, unmediated by professional interpreters. Exposure of the native population to Chinese literacy remained restricted to members of the ruling élite.[18] Unlike bureaucrats, Chinese merchants and money-lenders were more likely to learn to communicate in the local language, and there is fragmentary evidence of mixed marriages between Turki and Chinese.[19]

The sources
The task of preparing a study of the social role of literate and oral transmission in the 'traditional' social setting of Eastern Turkestan/Xinjiang is at present seriously hindered by the inaccessibility of archival materials and the restrictions on field work.[20] This paper is therefore no more than a

---

17. The Qing administration, like its modern Chinese counterpart, relied on local officials to manage the day-to-day affairs of the indigenous population. The fall of the Qing dynasty did not bring drastic interruptions to daily life. Indirect rule continued throughout the Republican period under Chinese warlords.
18. Cf. Goody 1977.
19. For references to such mixed unions under the Qing see Millward 1998: 206; for a later period see Skrine 1971: 203.
20. My field work in 1995 and 1996 in Southern Xinjiang was conducted under the close supervision of the local authorities, which seriously limited and hindered the acquisition of information. It was, for example, out of the question to ask about Sufi practices in contemporary society. Repeated requests to gain access to local archival materials, such as documents concerning marriage, divorce and inheritance from before 1949 were turned down by the Chinese research partners. As political tension in the province increased during the summer of 1996, it became impossible even to read local literary publications in Kashgar's public library, in spite of the fact that I had a research permit issued by the provincial authorities.

preliminary attempt to piece together fragmentary information about the Uyghur derived from a variety of non-Chinese sources.

As befits my subject matter, my data are based on written and oral sources. The written materials are a mixed bag, including travellers' accounts as well as indigenous texts. The travel literature dating from the second half of the nineteenth and the first half of the twentieth century is substantial, but it has only been sporadically used by researchers. I have argued elsewhere that, in spite of the typical 'orientalist' tendencies of many of these sources and their inherent romantic and patronising bias, there remain good grounds to take them seriously as ethnographic sources.[21] They are particularly important in view of the inaccessibility of local primary documents. The information provided by these sources often has an anecdotal character, as do details of an ethnographer's experiences. When combined and organised with other sources, however, even data such as these become useful.

In our case travellers' sources are augmented by native descriptions of local society from the same period. Some of these have been collected by European scholars as oral tradition or as linguistic specimens. Although transformed from oral performance into writing by outsiders, these texts constitute an important body of primary materials by local authors. In addition, I have used a group of texts, for the most part unpublished, which give valuable insight into local society, even though they were committed to paper at the request of members of the Swedish Mission and cannot be considered indigenous in the usual sense.

To the extent that our sources describe the assumptions that underpin everyday life, they can be considered ideal ethnographic materials. However, much of the local authors' social knowledge remains inevitably implicit. The materials do not list (let alone explain) all the normative rules of their society, and concrete accounts of social action are rare. This gap can be filled by travellers' descriptions and fieldwork,

---

21. Bellér-Hann 1996.

which often provide both illustrations and exceptions to normative rules articulated by these authors. Finally, by taking note of modern Uyghur ethnographic publications, it becomes possible to assemble at least a sketchy foundation for historical - anthropological analysis.

The plan of the paper is as follows. The main focus of Chapter One is on modes of transmission of knowledge among the Turki before they became the Uyghur, i.e. before the incorporation of Eastern Turkestan into communist China in 1949. It considers the role of the written word in daily life in traditional society. Special attention is paid to the role of the written word in communications with the supernatural. Chapter Two explores aspects of oral transmission in pre-modern society and argues, with a focus on the mixing of modes, that both oral and literate transmission were important. Chapter Three focuses on traditional, institutionalised forms of knowledge transmission, i.e. Islamic education. By the early twentieth century this was recognised by many to be backward and stagnant. As a result of the activities of some 'enlightened' individuals, efforts were made to reform and invigorate this antiquated education system. While the first three chapters are based on written sources, Chapter Four takes its materials from contemporary field work data. It highlights the persistence of patterns of transmission from pre-modern times, especially within small town and rural contexts. The argument centres on the opposing trends of state encouragement of secular mass literacy on the one hand and its perpetuation of oral modes of transmission on the other.

Chapter I. The written word before 1949

1. Economic transactions

Pre-1949 society was largely subsistence-oriented, although from the late nineteenth century onwards production for the market became increasingly important. Food production was highly dependent on weather conditions and the availability of water. Bad harvests caused food shortages or even famine. The availability of food was a central concern, and food itself had paramount importance in ritual exchange and in dealings with the supernatural.[22] Among Uyghur peasants in southern Xinjiang food-related metaphors are still commonly used to denote knowledge. Knowledgeable people, whether or not they have formal qualifications, are referred to in rural areas as people 'with cornmeal gruel in their belly' (*qosaqta umaç bar*), while an uncouth person is called 'black bellied' (*qaraqosaq*). This figurative congruence of food and knowledge is made possible through the association with energy, potency and creativity. Mohammad Ali Damolla, a local author writing at the beginning of the twentieth century, argued that knowledge became ripe (*pişşiq*) only through discussion.[23] Without discussion it remained raw, useless and poor. He also referred to the famous Sufi saint Ahmad Yasawi's poem, in which Paradise is assigned to knowledgeable people, while Hell is a place for the ignorant.

Knowledge and literacy were often considered synonymous and both commanded prestige and authenticity. The written word was particularly prominent in economic life. The Forsyth report in 1875 commented that exchanges of goods between merchants were occasionally made under written authority.[24] The source suggests that some written basis was customarily

---

22. Bellér-Hann forthcoming.
23. Prov.207.I.73.
24. Forsyth 1875: 482.

required between long-term trading partners whose commercial transactions exceeded ordinary caravan trade. At the time of the expedition's visit there were only three men in Kashgar and two in Yarkand who possessed sufficient capital to participate in such transactions. At the turn of the century banks were operating in the province, presumably for the convenience of travelling merchants. An indigenous source explains that the essence of banking was the profitable exchange of cash for unexpendable money *(nāqd sārplik pulni sārpsiz pulğa tegişip nāp aladur)*. Paper money was not accepted by shopkeepers and traders, but money-changers used it among themselves. Banks were needed because of the many different currencies that were circulating on the markets. Commission *(tapawāt)* was evidently charged. Many people kept their money in the bank because they were afraid of travelling with a lot of cash. After they had paid some money into the bank they received a receipt known as *dāstxeti* which they could present at the bank in another town and receive their money.[25]

Before 1949 the pawnbroker's shop was much frequented in Xinjiang.[26] An indigenous description of the institution explains how the system operated, and how heavily it depended on written evidence. The pawnbroker *(görākäş)* was a well-to-do merchant in possession of large amounts of cash. Those in need of cash took their valuables along to him. If a valuable was worth ten *tāñgā* then its owner would get a loan of two *misqal*.[27] These pawnbrokers were called *bir pulji*, because they took one *(bir) pul* per *tāñgā* interest each week for the money lent. Other pawnbrokers would give as much as

---

25. Such transactions also assumed a certain level of numerical skills. Prov.207.I.46.
26. Official pawnshops were set up soon after the Manchu invasion of the province in the eighteenth century. (Millward 1998: 84-5). According to informants in the 1990s, in the first half of the twentieth century pawnshops were operated by local Muslims, by Han Chinese and by Chinese Muslims.
27. Although *misqal* was a weight unit, in the 1930s it also referred to a silver coin weighing 3.5 grams and equalling 0.1 *sār*. (Schwarz 1992: 918).

five *tāṅgā* for something estimated to be worth ten *tāṅgā*. However, these asked for two (*iki*) *pul* interest for each *tāṅgā* lent, therefore they were known as *iki pulji*. The pawnbroker made out an initial letter in three copies to record the transaction. He gave one copy to the owner of the pawned object. The second copy was put aside with the object in question and the third copy was put into his [accounts] book, which was called *dañze*.[28] The pawnbroker would keep the pawned object for six months after which he could take it to the bazaar and sell it. If the customer lost his letter certifying the transaction, he had no right to reclaim the object. If another person happened to find this lost letter, he was expected to hand it to its owner. Occasionally stolen goods were taken to the pawnbroker's, who did not usually ask where the goods had come from.[29]

Property transactions also needed the written medium. We do not know how widespread the practice of applying for a certificate proving land ownership was but such certificates (*yār xeti*) were issued by courts and they were the only means of proving ownership. Only if one possessed such a certificate could one be confident of winning a dispute over the inheritance of land. Abdulqadir writing around 1930 in Yarkand describes how, when a man died, his family shared out his inheritance. To prevent later animosity, they could acquire a written document called *hōjjāt xeti* complete with the seal of a judge (*qazi*). This was sufficient to prevent other relatives later opening a lawsuit.[30] It has recently been claimed that most court cases in this period concerned inheritance of land.[31] The frequency of land disputes indicates that land ownership was not always documented, or if it was, the validity of the documentation could be questioned. A sophisticated technical vocabulary was used: *şcrakatnamā* was

---

28. Cf. Schwarz: *dañpuzul* <Chinese *dañ* =pawnshop (1992: 257).
29. Prov.207.I.45.
30. Prov.464.16V.
31. Nurhaji and Goguañ 1995: 357. I have not been able to consult the original Chinese source on which this claim is based.

a partnership agreement, the *baynamā* proved the deed of a sale, the *wākalatnamā* gave power of attorney to an appointed agent. Contracts for loans and mortgages were also codified in written form.³²

In line with common practice throughout the Islamic world, a person could decide to turn a piece of his land into a pious foundation *(waqf)* and allocate it to a mosque, a college (*mādrāsā*) or a shrine (*mazar*). In each case a document was drawn up, which was then sealed by a legal authority (*mufti* or *qazi*). This letter was then entrusted to the *imam* (leader of public worship) or the *xatip* (preacher). If the *waqf* was to belong to a shrine, then the document was handed over to the protégé of the *şāyx* (elder, Muslim scholar, here: the guardian) of the shrine. In this document it was stated that the *waqf* could not be sold, exchanged, changed, donated or pawned. The letter made out for the trustee specified that the foundation was made for God's sake (*sabil*).³³ The *şāyx* and *imam* of the institution acquired the right to cultivate the piece of land and to benefit from the harvest. Alternatively they could rent it out and use the proceeds. Our author suggests that some people used tricks (*hilā*) and abused the system by having these letters made out for ninety-nine years they sold this *waqf* property.³⁴

---

32. Examples of such documents are included in the Forsyth report, which also contains examples of certificates of purchase or possession of slaves, and the liberation of slaves. L/P & S/7/4. 1875, pp. 29-32. Oriental and Indian Office Library, London.
33. Cf. Schimmel 1990: 274.
34. Prov.207.I.66. Unfortunately our author talks about the *waqf* in general and remains too vague for us to draw any conclusions about the precise nature of the institution. According to Murat Çızakça the document gives the impression that a considerably stricter version of the *waqf* law was applied in Kashgar than in Ottoman lands. He also comments on the question of embezzlement, which may come about if the waqf is rented out. This would normally be applied if the buildings on the *waqf* land were dilapidated and needed urgent repairs. Long term renting of *waqf* property without such emergencies would imply embezzlement because it dilutes property rights. (Murat Çızakça personal communications.) For further details see Çızakça forthcoming.

2. *Dispute settlement*

Some disputes were resolved at court (*mähkimä*) in the course of lawsuits (*soraq*) which exposed both parties to the written word. In the *šari'ät* court the *qazi* and the *mufti* consulted legal books, and passed their judgement in accordance with the written word.[35] The typical procedure was as follows. First, a *mufti* prepared a formal legal opinion (*fatwa, pätiwa*) after consulting the relevant books. He wrote this on a piece of paper and put his seal on it. The *qazi* then formulated his decision according to the *fatwa*.[36] When a plaintiff approached a *mufti* with the aim of obtaining a *fatwa* in a certain case, the *mufti* did not ask him to produce evidence to prove the truthfulness of his words; he accepted his verbal account and issued the *fatwa* on the basis of this (*aġzidin çiqqan sözniñ bayaniġa qaylap fatwa qilip bärädür*).[37]

Disputes could also be settled out of court by the writing of an agreement (*razinamä*).[38] Civil court cases were

---

35. Handbooks of Hanafite law.
36. This passage follows our indigenous author, Mohammad Ali Damolla's description of normative practice rather than the reality of any concrete case. However, legally speaking, the *qazi* was not obliged to follow the *fatwa* when formulating his judgement.
37. Prov.207.I.47. Nevertheless, elsewhere the same author confirms that it was necessary to take an oath (*qäsäm*) if someone was not believed. For example, when two adversaries went to the qazi and one claimed that the other owed him a certain sum but refused to pay his debt, the other could say that he had already paid his debt. In such a case the taking of an oath was considered necessary. If a person insisted that his adversary should take an oath, then it was accepted that the adversary was right. If he claimed however, that he had already paid his debt, then it was his adversary's turn to take an oath after which the latter received his money. If a person had someone else's money without a legal document (*wäsiqä*) he could not receive his money without taking an oath. If he had two witnesses to prove his case, no oath was required. If the witnesses took an oath, the person would receive his money. (Prov.207.I.52.)
38. L/P & S/7/4. 1875, p. 29. Oriental and Indian Office Library, London.

recorded, with date, the names of the adversaries, the nature of their dispute, the names of witnesses and the judgement passed. An example of such records comprising cases from the late nineteenth century was acquired by Martin Hartmann in Kashgar in 1902.[39]

3. Marriage and divorce

Forsyth mentions the necessity of obtaining written documents before contracting a marriage. 'When the marriage terms are agreed to, the girl's parents get a letter of permit from the governor of the city to the effect that „such a one, the daughter of so and so, son of so and so, of such a place, marries with their consent such a one, the son of so and so, of such a place."'[40] The fee for this letter of permit and registry was one *tāṅgä* (which at Forsyth's time was worth about sixpence) to the city governor. The practice is mentioned only in the urban context and we have no way of knowing to what extent it was observed in rural areas. Other foreign observers in the early twentieth century also confirm that a written permission for marriage had to be obtained from the local *bäg*, who issued it for a small fee. Furthermore, the same observers claim that a certificate from the *imam* of the neighbourhood was also needed to prove that the woman was free to marry.[41] Thus, in principle at least, marriage required the written approval of both the local secular and religious authorities.

The instability of the institution of marriage among the settled population in the province was proverbial among foreign visitors.[42] Travellers in the late nineteenth century refer to the necessity of acquiring a written document (*talaqnamā*, or *talaq xāt*) from the Islamic court as proof of divorce. According to Forsyth, 'the ceremony of divorce

---

39. 2 3296. Hartmann Sammlung, Staatsbibliothek zu Berlin. I am grateful to Mr. Jun Sugawara for drawing my attention to this document.
40. Forsyth 1875: 84.
41. Sykes & Sykes 1920: 311.
42. For a detailed account see Benson 1993b.

amounts to no more than the affixing of the cazi's seal to the talaknamas, which are kept one by the man, and one by the woman, in proof of their release from the marriage tie.'[43] Linguistic evidence also implies that the written documentation of divorce was common practice. In southern Xinjiang today, especially in rural areas, the colloquial expressions used to refer to divorce use a metaphor embedded in literacy. When a man wants to say that he has divorced his wife, he says 'I have given her her letter' [of divorce] (*xetini bärdim*), a woman would say 'I have taken my letter' [of divorce] (*xetimni aldim*). To express intention of divorce (in jest or as a threat), the same expressions are used in the present tense. My own observations confirm that while marriage is considered the normal state of life, divorce in southern Xinjiang does not carry any particular stigma, and women, both in rural areas and in the cities, do their best to remarry following divorce. Based on my informants' reminisces and on travel accounts, it is reasonable to assume that the situation was not very different before 1949. Obtaining written evidence of divorce was, especially for a woman, an indispensable condition of remarriage. The document clearly stated the woman's altered family status and it had to state the time of divorce. One hundred days had to elapse between her divorce and remarriage, as prescribed by Islamic law, to ensure knowledge of the paternity of a child in case of pregnancy.

4. *Private communication*

The written medium was used outside the realms of formal legal and commercial activities. Merchants and traders, who had to travel long distances and be away from their home for long periods, kept in touch with their families through correspondence. Although we do not know when exactly this

---

43. Forsyth 1875: 90. The Forsyth report produces examples of both marriage and divorce contracts from Kashgar .L/P & S/7/4. 1875, p. 28. Oriental and Indian Office Library, London.

exchange of private messages in written form became widespread and how common it was in the beginning of the century, we know that it was common enough by the 1930s for the Swedish Mission's Printing Press to publish a booklet giving examples of letters in the Turki language.[44] Most people, non-literate or with a limited degree of literacy, had their messages written for them by a professional scribe, the *xätçi/xät pütükçi*. He was told the contents of the intended message orally, after which he could compose the letter, following some unwritten rules and using a number of set formulae. Letters were then put in Chinese or European envelopes. Well-to-do non-literates sealed their letters, while poor people used their right thumb for signature.[45] However, such practices were clearly not uniform, since a local source reports that when a professional scribe copied a letter, he could sign the letter himself.[46]

5. *Popular practices*

Certain popular practices in pre-modern times also made use of writing. The 'snow game' was usually acted out to mark the falling of the first snow. Like most other rituals, it centred on hospitality. The decision as to whose obligation it was going to be to offer food and hospitality to kin and friends was made as a result of a challenge. The challenger and the challenged had to be more or less social equals, both capable of offering the same level of hospitality. The challenger visited his friend when the first snow had fallen and left behind in his house a verse (*qar xät*) explaining the necessity of organising a winter banquet and offering him a challenge to catch him. If the person thus challenged found this note quickly and could catch the author of the note before he reached his own home, then the challenger was made up, and, dressed as a woman,

---

44. *Xutut* 1937. For an earlier example of a private letter sent by a woman to her husband who had gone to Mecca see Vámbéry 1865.
45. Le Coq 1916: 5.
46. Prov.207.I.50.

paraded through the streets. In addition, he had to organise a banquet for friends and acquaintances. But if the challenger could reach his home without being caught, the receiver of the poem had to organise the feast within a week. If the invitations did not arrive by the expected time, he was warned that further delays would bring calamity to him, because his door would be blocked by a bier. Jarring has published such a *qar xät*, which he obtained in 1929 from a *molla*:

'God, may He be exalted, through his mercy gave us the snow,
For this reason let us meet brothers and friends.
If, with some excuse, they catch the one who brought the snow (-letter)
he has to put cups and pots and sweets on a tray.[47]

Reciting passages from literary works was an important part of the *mäṣräp*, the traditional male social gathering, the privilege of the rich and well-to-do. The works recited here were the well-known Islamic works widespread in Central Asia, and included those by Rabğuzi Attar, Jami and Firdawsi, as well as the writings of mystic authors such as Yasawi, his disciple Suläyman Bakirğan, and the Şäyx Allayar. Furthermore, the various exploits of Muslim heroes descended from Ali were also popular.[48]

The recitation of written works did not exclude various forms of verbal arts. Improvised jokes and humorous verbal exchanges also formed an important part of the entertainment provided during the *mäṣräp* by some of the participants.[49]

Literacy in most of the above cases remained restricted to certain groups: the *mäṣräp* was the prerogative of men belonging to the well-to-do classes, the snow-game assumed a

---

47. Jarring 1975: 14-5.
48. Pantusov 1907: 10-12; 5-6.
49. Prov. 207.1.13. For descriptions of and references to the institution of the *mäṣräp* see Jarring 1975: 15-8; Roberts 1998; Bellér-Hann 1998; Raxman et al. 1996: 144-7; Häbibulla 1993: 448-59.

certain level of economic well-being, landless peasants could not always have recourse to courts, etc. Gender, economic position, social prestige, residence, level of schooling and many other factors must have influenced the actual use of writing. However, the activities of the more privileged social groups remained under the close scrutiny of poorer people who usually aspired to emulate their social superiors. Participation in the above mentioned activities accentuated social difference but these activities were known to everyone. Marriage and divorce, disputes, visits to the pawnbrokers' shops and other commercial transactions concerned men and women, and more than just the privileged segments of the population. Regardless of whether they actually made use of written documents for confirmation and authorisation of contracts, there was general awareness of the resources offered by literacy. Anybody could watch the book-peddlers do business, or listen to the tales in the bazaar of storytellers who drew on a book source for increased authenticity. Many attended the local primary schools, or at least knew others who had spent some time in school to acquire basic literacy skills. All men, including the dispossessed, beggars and labourers, were given the honourable title of *axun*, literally 'reader of the Koran', regardless of their actual literacy skills.[50] This title persists in modern Uyghur rural society. It implies high prestige for literacy and religious learning (often perceived as synonymous) and it also points to hierarchically ordered gender relations by implying that knowledge and literacy are male attributes *per se*. However, in pre-1949 society girls were just as likely to attend primary school as boys, albeit for shorter periods. This normative association of men with literacy and knowledge is, therefore, best seen as an other example of how patriarchal values are emphasised while women's assertive participation and active presence in all areas of social life is consistently played down.[51]

---

50. Nazaroff 1935: 48.
51. See Bellér-Hann 1998a.

6. *Literacy and beliefs*

In modern societies literacy is generally considered as both an important indicator of development, and one of the most effective means to achieve it. It is perhaps the most influential weapon against ignorance which is often equated with superstition.[52] In this light it may appear ironic that the one area of everyday life in which people from all walks of life came into contact with the written word was negotiations with the supernatural world. This use of writing must be distinguished from its use to disseminate normative religious knowledge, which was closely tied to traditional *mäktäp* education and presupposed some degree of literacy skills. Non-literate people often made direct use of the written word. In studying the role of writing in West Africa, Jack Goody noted that 'the initial appeal of Islam to outsiders was frequently magical, and that writing was at first valued more for its role in superhuman than in human communication'.[53] Superstition, often defined as the antithesis of literacy, also made good use of the prestige and power attributed to the written word in the England of the Industrial Revolution.[54]

In the early twentieth century in Xinjiang literacy was by and large associated with religious specialists. Respect for literacy was closely connected to respect for and fear of the supernatural. The Russian exile Nazaroff reports that in the streets and bazaars of Yarkand numerous wooden boxes were used for the reception of waste paper. Paper was the medium for the writing of the word of God, and so it had to be collected and protected from use for any unclean purpose.[55] Chinese presence in the bazaars reinforced this respect

---

52. For an elaborate discussion of the dichotomy between literate knowledge and superstition see Vincent 1989: 156-76.
53. Goody 1987: 133.
54. Vincent 1989: 156-175.
55. Nazaroff 1935: 134.

accorded to the written word and paper in general, since in the opinion of the English missionaries 'it was the old Chinese Confucianist, omnipresent in every bazaar, who collected pieces of paper lying about, putting them in special baskets.' The sacred papers were then taken to temples to be burnt by the priest.⁵⁶ However, this reverence was not always unqualified. When Christian missionaries distributed religious booklets and Turki translations of Bible portions, local people would tear up or burn them. Later, however, at least according to missionary reports, they were happy to buy them and showed them the same reverence Muslims showed to holy writings. An estimated 60,000 -70,000 religious booklets were sold or distributed free during the time of the Swedish mission's work in the province during the first half of the twentieth century.⁵⁷ When the Scottish missionary, George Hunter presented a man called Toqsun molla an Arabic New Testament, the recipient „buried his face in the book and kissed it".⁵⁸ But the same author also tells us how he had often seen Turkis '...buy gospels and tracts specially to tear up in one's presence or to burn publicly on the main street. Should anyone seem to show interest in a Gospel or tract, others will come and say - *Bismillah Yok* (There is no *Bismillah*) and otherwise seek to discourage a would be purchaser. It is not an uncommon thing for an absolutely illiterate man to come forward and ask to look at a tract and all unconscious that he is holding it upside down, he pretends to read it, then before the crowd of onlookers he hands back the tract with utter disdain, saying, Bismillah Yok.'⁵⁹

Among the indigenous population there was general awareness of the centrality of the Koran and of Muslims being one of the peoples of the book. However, few people possessed a Koran and not all who possessed it could read it.

---

56. Cable & French 1942: 192.
57. Hultvall 1981: 5. For references to the Christian literature circulated by missionaries in the province see Hunter 1920.
58. Hunter 1907: 46.
59. Hunter 1920: 168-9.

Furthermore, most of those who could read the Arabic script could not understand the Arabic language in which it was written. However, contact with the holy book was possible not only through reading and studying it, which before the development of printing and mass literacy remained largely restricted to learned *mādrāsā* scholars.

Most people would come into direct contact with the Koran through its magical use by the fortune-teller. S/he was also visited when something in the house went missing. Although various other methods of soothsaying were also used, according to Katanov in the end of the nineteenth century in Eastern Turkestan using the Koran was the most widespread technique.[60] The client was asked to close his/her eyes and the Koran was put into his/her hands. Starting from the page where the Koran was opened, seven pages were turned, and on this page the seventh line was found and the diviner said something like 'if your lost property is not found today, it will be found tomorrow. If not tomorrow, then the day after tomorrow'. After this he prayed.[61] Methods of soothsaying with the Koran were codified and circulated in book form. Katanov reproduced a text as it had been dictated to him on the 6th April 1892 in Turfan by Mullah Xoja-Nay-xan, son of Memet-Maqsud Bek, who was born in 1827. He learnt soothsaying with the Koran from a book entitled *Falnamā*, which had belonged to a fortune-teller called Abdulrahim from Turfan. Abdulrahim's method was demonstrated to Katanov by Nay-xan. The oracle consisted of thirty-seven sheets with eleven lines on each. 'We take the Koran and, closing our eyes, we say „I have set my hopes on God". We hold the Koran level with our head, with its back to our nose. If it is morning, we open it in the beginning, at lunch time we open it somewhere in the middle and in the evening somewhere in the end. Then we turn seven pages towards the right hand side [the beginning]. On the right page we count seven lines and look at the first letter of the seventh line.'

---

60. Katanov 1894.
61. Katanov - Menges 1933: 1250-3.

Each letter was attributed a different meaning and could be interpreted according to need. For instance, the first letter of the Arabic alphabet, *ālip*, was interpreted as the oracle of the Holy Adam and therefore as a good omen in all things.[62]

This example, in which different parts of the Koran were equated with different parts of the day, shows how literacy contributed to forms of symbolism. Symbolic significance could also be attributed to the shape of the letters of the Arabic alphabet which, according to the testimony of a proverb, could be interpreted as representing moral behaviour.

'If you are upright like an *ālif*, you will never be exposed to calamity. If you are crooked like (the combination of) *ālif lam*, all kinds of calamity will be your lot.'[63]

Other types of hand-written books which served magical purposes also circulated. These works known as *Sa'atnamā* ('Books of the hour') aimed at assisting people to avoid bad luck and misfortune. Since not all could afford to possess and read such a book, and because very old copies could become unusable, the transmission of the contents of such a work could become entirely oral. Katanov's informant, Nay-xan dictated the contents of such a book from memory (Turfan in 1892). It explained the auspicious and inauspicious nature of each day of the month. For example, the first day of the month was considered auspicious, because that was the day that Adam was created. If one wished anything from God on this day it was bound to be granted, and it was also auspicious for visiting superiors, for business, for building houses. Moreover, a child born on such a day was predicted to become rich and a great man.[64]

---

62. Katanov 1894. The use of the Koran and other sacred texts for magical purposes, such as divination, was widespread also elsewhere in the Islamic world. Strictly speaking, only the use of secular, poetical texts for the same purpose was called *fāl*. (Rypka 1959: 521-2). In Iran the poetry collection of Hafiz was widely used for divination in a fashion very similar described above (Browne 1920: 311-319).
63. Jarring 1985: 49.
64. Katanov - Menges 1976: 96-9.

Also at the end of the nineteenth century, the Russian researcher Pantusov acquired a manuscript in Verny (modern Almaty), the contents of which were comparable to the account of Katanov's informant. This text was written in a dialect characteristic of the Turki inhabitants of the Ili region in Northern Xinjiang, also known as the Taranchi. This was entitled *Sa'atnamā* of the Aqsaqal Qurban Niyaz. The details of the text correspond to the oral information dictated to Katanov by his informant in Turfan, although deviations from this written account are also numerous. Special attention was paid to the days when blood should not be taken; to how the day on which a baby is born could influence the child's character. Furthermore, the suitability of different days for making wishes, taking medication, building or moving house, sowing seeds, engaging in business, pursuing a craft and even planting a tree also figured in the account.[65]

To what extent such books were regularly consulted is not known, but sources agree that there was a general awareness of their existence. Members of the British Forsyth mission in the late nineteenth century commented how the day of the circumcision ceremony for boys was fixed only after consulting the stars and a book of lucky days and omens, in which every day of every month had its special prognostic qualities.[66] But the German archaeologist Le Coq found that, although omens and dream interpretations were well-known, people did not appear to attribute great importance to them.[67]

Knowledge of the suitability of certain activities on certain days was not restricted to the uneducated. Indigenous authors in the first half of the twentieth century, themselves learned religious teachers, included similar information in their essays on local culture commissioned by members of the Swedish Mission. Particularly rich in this type of information is Molla Abdulqadir's work written in Yarkand around 1930. He relates how it was considered lucky to give birth on a Sunday,

---

65. Pantusov 1897.
66. Forsyth 1875: 87.
67. Le Coq 1916: 5.

Friday, Saturday or Wednesday because such days would have a positive influence on the baby's character, but to give birth on a Tuesday and at the end of the year was regarded as inauspicious.[68] Friday was auspicious for distributing alms, to visit sick people and parents, to cut out clothes and shoes etc. But the same day was considered bad for sowing seeds and irrigating the land, or for loading threshed grain.[69] In summertime peasants tended to do the loading of their threshed grain on a Tuesday because on this day the Prophet Xizir was said to watch over the threshing from a tree.[70]

Swedish mission reports contain further references to the wide circulation of this type of knowledge, e.g. that to die on Friday was considered very fortunate but on Wednesday it was supposed to be dangerous because on this day the gates of Hell stood open. 'Each month has unlucky days when no work should be undertaken but three are especially critical. The most critical is the first day of each month.'[71]

Pantusov followed his publication of the book of lucky and unlucky days with the reproduction and translation of a book of auspicious and unlucky years. In this each year of the twelve year calendar cycle used by Turkic and Mongolian peoples is considered separately. Not only people's bodily characteristics but also their fate was supposed to be determined by the year they were born in. For example, those born in the year of the Mouse would be white-faced with black hair. Regardless whether he had been rich or poor before, after the age of forty he will get rich.[72]

There are numerous other examples of the magical use of the written word. In Turfan men and women used to gather on the 7th, the 17th and the 27th of the month of Säpär, with the purpose to pray for good luck. On the night of the seventh

---

68. Prov.464.13R.
69. Prov.464.4V.
70. Prov.464.10R. On Xizir (Khidr) see Franke, forthcoming.
71. Jarring 1979: 15. Attributing special significance to certain times was of course well-known elsewhere in the Islamic world, see for example Westermarck 1926: 132-134.
72. Pantusov 1901.

ceremonial food was prepared and an important part of the ritual was when the religious specialist, the *molla* came and read the Book of Good Fortune (*Bäxtnamä*) which took about two hours.[73] The power of the written word was considered strong enough to recover hidden treasure, to render sterile marriages fertile, to manipulate love. For such purposes amulets of all sorts were used, which could be a small coin, a jade stone, some fruit or bread, or a piece of paper with writing on it (*tumar*).[74] Any of these could make the indifferent fall in love, which was called *isitma* (heating), or, conversely could render people indifferent towards their beloved, which was known as *soğutma* (cooling). Black magic was also exercised with the aid of writing. The sorcerer took a piece of thread as long as the height of the person to be affected. He then fixed a piece of paper to it with cabalistic formulae scribbled over it. This had to be buried in the cemetery, and by the time the thread rotted away, the person would die.[75]

The above examples illustrate that learned *mollas* were well-informed of magical practices current among the population, and this knowledge, regardless whether they approved of the practices or not, rendered them mediators between the 'great' and the 'little' traditions. At least one early source implies that writing could be used as a means of communication between members of the religious classes and saints. Mirza Haydar, writing in the sixteenth century, mentions the magical practice connected to one of the saintly tombs in Kashgar. '....a hole has been made in his grave opposite to where his face is. No change has taken place: his beard is [still] perfectly straight, and he is recognisable. I have heard the Ulama of Káshghar say that whenever they had a difficult question to decide, they would write a copy of it and place it in the tomb; on the morrow, when they came, they

---

73. Katanov-Menges 1976: 62-5.
74. For the widespread use of amulets elsewhere in the Islamic world see for example Schimmel 1990: 264-266,
75. Grenard 1898a: 256-7.

found the answer written down. And this has been tried and tested. (The responsibility be upon their shoulders.)'[76] In a rare work on Central Asian hagiography it is related that, following the death of the mystic Muhibb Khumar, his snake continued to act as a doorkeeper. 'People would come with their problems, leave some paper and ink, and return later to find written answers. This went on for 200 years. Twenty years after Muhibb's death the snake also died. A written answer instructed the local people to bury it in the *langar*.'[77]

However, the written word was also influenced by local Islamic knowledge and at the same time informed it. Pantusov himself explains that some of the *naxşa* are expressions of *hikmāt* (wisdom) derived from Koranic verses.[78] Guidebooks teaching the basic tenets of Islam, moral conduct, narratives of saints' lives, poetry, love stories and cautionary tales were occasionally committed to writing and circulated first in hand-written, later in lithographed and printed editions.[79] The greater part of Eastern Turki literature available to the literate part of the Kashgari population belonged to the category of history, classical Arabic and Persian literature in translation and Islamic theological and philosophical-moralising literature, most of which had been translated from Arabic and Persian.[80] The hand-written Islamic works mostly available in Khotan before the 1860s were saintly legends and Koran

---

76. Haidar 1895: 301.
77. Baldick 1993: 165. For a critique of Baldick's work see DeWeese 1996.
78. Pantusov 1890: xv-xvi.
79. Nur Hajjim, a taylor from Yangi Hisar had learnt the art of lithography in North West India. In Kashgar he printed Turki poetry as well as Chinese works such as an instruction book for soldiers in 4000 copies upon orders from Urumchi. (Hartmann 1904: 75-6). The Swedish missionaries operated their printing press from 1912. (Hultvall 1981: 5). In the 1930s the press of the Swedish Mission in Kashgar printed newspapers, political pamphlets and even banknotes for the insurgent Turks. In 1933 the press of the former Swedish Mission at Yarkand was taken over by the authorities of the Turkish Islamic Republic of Eastern Turkestan and radical Islamic literature in support of the new state was printed on it including the journal *Istiqlal* (Jarring 1974: 265; Forbes 1986: 114).
80. Jarring 1980.

commentaries.[81] Grenard reports that at the end of the nineteenth century tales, mostly translated from Persian, often circulated in book form. Such tales were often recited by story tellers who attracted large crowds of listeners in the bazaar.[82] In the second half of the nineteenth century Dr Bellew visited the book-shops of Yarkand. He found mostly Turki manuscripts on religious subjects and some lithographed books on medicine, history and theology written in Persian. Local historical records and specimens of native literature were said to have been kept in dervish compounds attached to shrines or in the possession of private individuals.[83] Hartmann noted that reading ('Buchwesen') in the region was on a very low level.[84] Indirect evidence suggests that there must have been a small circle of people whose linguistic abilities also included some knowledge of Persian although we do not know to what extent this readership belonged to the local, indigenous population or to the numerous foreigners residing in the cities. A thorough knowledge of the Arabic language was limited to the educated élite. Most people could recite some Koranic verses in Arabic, albeit without understanding them. Pantusov recorded the words of a blind beggar, who, in addition to requesting passers-by in Turki also recited a tradition in Arabic.[85] Although copies of books were sometimes made, the making of copies was laborious and expensive.[86]

---

81. Grenard 1898b: 85-6.
82. Grenard 1898b: 85-6.
83. Bellew 1875: 278.
84. 1904: 74.
85. Pantusov 1890: 71, 153.
86. An indigenous essay dating from the early years of the twentieth century elaborating on the making of copies reasons, that copies were made when the original book became very old or when multiple copies were needed. This was also done when documents had to be drawn up: when a person submitted a request, an unsealed copy of the original document was attached to the application which then had to be matched to the original, sealed copy. A copy was also necessary in case the original, sealed version got lost. (Prov.207.I.50.)

Summary

Pre-modern, pre-industrial societies, such as Eastern Turkestan was before 1949, are associated with low literacy rates. It is often assumed that oral transmission dominated over literacy and that writing was the domain of a privileged few. This was no doubt true for the region under discussion. Nonetheless, in spite of high levels of illiteracy, Turki, especially in urban areas, had direct contact with the written word, regardless of whether they themselves could read and write. Eastern Turkestan had a rich history of various religions and literate traditions even before the advent of Islam. Foreign dominance brought with it a long history of bureaucratic and literate tradition and superficial exposure to Confucianism confirmed a reverence for the written word that was also central to Islam. Islam, as a 'religion of the book' introduced a new script and writing tradition from the West, which not only promoted a literate culture among an educated elite but also fostered general awareness of literacy in daily life. Certain forms of economic transaction, divorce and other legal decisions were made according to the norms of Muslim jurisprudence. The Islamic tradition exerted its influence throughout the society. Popular-magical practices common elsewhere in the Islamic world made ample use of the written word to mediate hidden knowledge and as a means to influence the future. Although the prestige attributed to writing was closely connected to the centrality of the Koran and reverence for it, informal dealings with the supernatural brought people with limited or zero literacy skills into direct contact with the written word. At the same time, religious knowledge was also informed by works translated into Turki from Persian and Arabic, which represented genres and contents well-known all over the Islamic world.

Chapter II. Oral solutions and the interface between oral and written transmission

1. The oral option

In the previous chapter, using fragmentary and scattered information committed to writing by indigenous authors and foreign observers I assessed the significance of the written word in traditional Uyghur society. However, it became apparent that the discussion is incomplete without references to oral modes of transmission. The written word was seldom if ever the only source of authenticity. On the contrary, written authorisation was an option which coexisted and constantly mingled with oral forms.

In the *mäşräp* oral recitation of written works paralleled textual study, and this mingling of the two forms of transmission was typical of traditional Islamic education. Commercial transactions did not necessarily require written documentation. In dispute settlement written authority had no universal superiority over oral forms. Disputes could be solved without recourse to a literate tradition. Grenard, writing at the end of the nineteenth century, implies that traditional dispute settlement was entirely oral. It took place in the public sphere, namely in the street, and involved a 'Homeric exchange' of mutual verbal abuse between the adversaries on the basis of unwritten but effectively institutionalised rules. The neighbours surrounded them and watched the scene, but would interfere only if violence was used. In such a case the person who had struck was told: 'you have done an improper thing (*namaqol*), now you must say that you are sorry (*namaqol bol*). The offender then offered his pipe to his adversary who accepted it, which concluded the affair. Although the scene in the street could be avoided, the affair was usually concluded with the pipe ceremony which was organised through the mediation of respected members of the community.[87] Confirmation of this pattern of out-of-court dispute settlement comes from Raquette, according to whom '...in reconciliation

---

87. Grenard 1898a:144-5.

ceremonies, whichever party has to give way in the dispute must invite the other party to tea. In Yarkand it also happens in lesser disputes that the water pipe was substituted for tea (*çilim tutmaq*)'.[88] That the water-pipe and the teacup were instrumental in out-of-court, oral dispute settlement is further confirmed by Jarring, who explains that 'one of the two had to be made available for such purposes: the person who has been wronged had to be offered tea or a pipe by the offender (his opponent). The ensuing reconciliation apparently had much more force than a written agreement and many solemn words.'[89]

Although marriage and divorce in principle required documentation, we cannot be sure how often these expectations were met in practice. Some sources emphasise only the verbal nature of the ceremony. In connection with the institution of temporary marriage, Nazaroff remarks that after the wedding feast 'the mullah reads the ceremony of divorce in advance, to simplify matters'.[90] Since for all written documents a small fee was demanded, we can speculate that the poorest could not always afford to acquire written documents. In some rural areas, which constituted small scale, face-to-face communities, such evidence was probably less often needed than in the urban environment, where oral forms of social control in the form of gossip were often insufficient to keep individuals' movements in check.

In dealings with the supernatural oral modes of communication paralleled the written form. As elsewhere in the Islamic world, curses and blessings were regarded as effective, and spells were particularly feared. Food was not only used in metaphors of knowledge; it could also be used to convey messages. Le Coq reports the following from the early twentieth century. Since most women could neither read nor write, their love affairs had to be conducted using another method which essentially served as a substitute for a love

---

88. Raquette 1909: 22.
89. Jarring 1975: 18.
90. Nazaroff 1935: 25.

letter. Le Coq's servant, the twenty-four year old Yusup received such a message from the daughter of a rich peasant. The message itself took the form of a small bag containing a number of objects and items of food, each one of them conveying a different meaning. When Le Coq recommended that the foodstuff at least could be consumed, Yusup rejected the idea vehemently, saying that, since it was quite possible that the woman had magical formulae recited over these objects, consuming the food could render him dependent on her.[91]

In other words, the cases cited in Chapter One to demonstrate the importance of the written form of communication turn out on closer inspection to be illustrations of the interface of the written and the oral. In this chapter I wish to look more closely at the role of oral transmission of knowledge in pre-1949 Uyghur society. Once again we find subtle mingling and interconnectedness, a permanent two-way traffic between the two domains.

2. The mixing of modes

Collecting folklore materials among the Taranchi in the north of the province in 1881-2, Pantusov noted legends about folk heroes and Muslim saints, historical songs, erotic and wedding songs (*ōläñ*), songs for healing (*awa, sänäm*), songs of mendicants, and lullabies.[92] *Ğärib Sännäm Şah*, a popular folk story in prose with lyrical parts, was often performed, especially during the wintertime in such a way that part of the prose was recited, and two other persons would then sing the verses to the accompaniment of the *dutar*, a plucked, two-stringed instrument. A particularly well known performer of this piece was a certain Imr Hāsān, who lived in the small village of Tazğun situated between Yangi Hissar and Kashgar.[93]

---

91. Le Coq 1928: 89-91.
92. Pantusov 1890: xv-xvi.
93. Jarring 1933: 5.

The technique of memorising formed an essential part of both formal and informal learning. It did not necessarily assume literate knowledge: knowledge acquired through oral transmission, which characterised elementary education, too, was equally recognised. As mentioned above, Hāmār Waki, Radloff's Taranchi informant dictated a number of texts from memory in 1862-3, which he had heard recited by *mollas*.[94] No doubt, such texts were reworked through the process of reproduction and thus the performers themselves must have played an important role in shaping the texts.

Some stories and songs which circulated in book form which were performed in public by story tellers and singers were translated or composed by *mollas*. Performers could include translations of literary pieces and the texts did not necessarily represent the language of the people. Among the songs, which Grenard and his companions heard, some were adaptations from the books of Ahmād and Yusuf. Particularly popular were stories of Mäşräb, the merry dervish, the impudent mendicant, perhaps the most popular among all Turkestani saints.[95] In November 1902 Martin Hartmann, the German scholar, met two male singers (aged 15, and 25 respectively) whose main piece was a song about Husayn's martyrdom at Kerbela. In Yarkand he met another male singer who knew the same song. Apparently, this man had learnt it from his father. This singer also knew that this song had been composed by a Mollah Kiçik about a hundred years before (cca 1800) who lived in Keriya (south of the Taklamakan desert in Eastern Turkestan) by the Shrine of Imam Ja'far al-Sadiq.[96] The Swedish missionary-surgeon, Gustav Raquette reports a tradition, which was current at the time of his stay in the province among the people of Yarkand. It concerned the origins of the city. He heard the story from an old, trustworthy

---

94. Radloff 1886: IV.
95. Grenard 1898b: 80-1.
96. Hartmann 1908: 40-41. This is a nice example of the appropriation and integration of Islamic tradition into local lore. Imam Ja'far al-Sadiq was the last Imam who died in Medina and was subsequently buried there.

person, who in his youth had read 'a very old manuscript, now quite lost, in which this tradition was written down.'[97]

Some popular pieces were adaptations from elsewhere. The German archaeologist Le Coq published such a poem, which apparently enjoyed great popularity in Qaraxoja. He noted that the language was not the vernacular spoken in the area, and his informants were unable to explain several passages. He concluded that the poem originated in Western Turkestan and was most probably a literary composition.[98]

Some songs and poems were not exclusively performed in Turki. Hartmann heard of a man who knew many songs about the Tungan-Chinese wars, many of them composed in half-Turki, half-Chinese.[99] Based on such fragmentary information, we can assume that there was a considerable mixing of the written and the oral modes of transmission, of diverse cultural and even linguistic traditions.[100]

Prestige was usually accorded to the written word. This prestige at least partially derived from the close associations made between literacy and its use in the religious/magical domains. Religious knowledge presupposed some connection to literacy, and basic literacy was often manifested in an ability to recite some Koranic verses. In fact, the concept of knowledge probably overlapped to some extent with literate knowledge. Such inter-connections are illustrated by the expressions common today among townspeople and rural residents in Southern Xinjiang, who use the word *sawat* ('literacy', 'schooling', 'education') also to mean 'culture' and 'knowledge'. A person who is described as *sawadi bar kişi* could be a literate or a cultured person.[101] Someone who is regarded as *dindin sawadi bar kişi* is a person with a certain degree of religious knowledge or education. Religious/literate knowledge could be demonstrated in the form of oral

---

(Halm 1988: 37).
97. Raquette 1909: 21.
98. Le Coq 1911: 66-7.
99. Hartmann 1908: 40-41.
100. For similar developments elsewhere see e.g. Vincent 1989: 199.

transmission, i.e. in public or communal recitals. The Khotanese Nur Luke reports about the commemoration of death (*näzir-çiraq*) organised on the fortieth day following death. On this occasion the expenses were considerable and each invited (male) guest was expected to donate twice or three times the amount of money than the value of the food he had consumed. He handed it over to the person responsible for the funeral (*ōlūkniñ igisi*), saying *qirq qutluğluqi*. This money had to be given by all those participants who were unable to recite ten to twenty verses (*ayāt*) from the Koran. Those who could, recited the verses and were exempted from payment.[102] Evidently, knowledge of and ability to recite Koranic verses had almost measurable value.

At the same time some types of knowledge must have carried higher prestige than others and respect for the written word did not go completely unchallenged. Although law was intimately connected to religion and religious practitioners, the formalities of legal documents (and possibly the judgements themselves) could invite ridicule. The Swedish missionary-surgeon Raquette obtained the following 'document' in 1908 in the bazaar of Yarkand 'where it went from man to man and was read with universal amusement.' Raquette claims that this humorous parody of a legal document faithfully reflects the then current legal style:

'In the year one thousand three hundred and twenty-five, the month räjäb the sixth. I, who am Muhammad Niaz Axon, from the quarter Quruq-köl-bash, little beard, medium sized, Muhammed Kurban Khuja's son, have (herewith) made open, legal and judicial acknowledgement, that I am indebted ten kicks, four boxes on the ear, ten cuts with a whip, ten blows with a stick, five blows with a fist to Roze Axon, from the quarter of Aq-mesjed, uncle Kurban Bay's son. The aforesaid boxes on the ear, kicks, cuts with a whip, blows with a stick (and) blows with a fist I have undertaken within the course of

---

101. Schwarz 1992: 457-8.
102. Prov.212:86-88.

a month, not making legal process, to pay in full. (His Mark).

Five ringdoves, four crows, ten sparrows, four hoopoes, two quails are witnesses.'[103]

Oral and written were intimately interconnected, and, as the above examples illustrate, both were closely tied to public performance. Reading was regarded as a primarily oral skill which also implicitly assumed an audience rather than a silent, individual act. A description of reading from the early twentieth century by a local *molla* supports this assumption.

'When reading, the greatest thing is the fact that one has to put one's heart and soul into it and read with all one's heart. If one does it only with the power of one's eyes, little comes out of it. Often, when someone's mind is somewhere else but his eyes are with the script, other words emerge from his mouth.'[104] Furthermore, our author remarks about the conditions of reading as follows:

'When reading, do not make a habit of bringing the script very close to your eyes. If you say „I shall read holding it far away", it cannot be read. And do not make it a habit to move your head to and fro when reading. It is considered a fault. The habit you first acquire when reading, you will (always) practice [sic!]. Another condition is this: Don't read letting the end of one word come into contact with the following word. Read every word to the end and stop for a moment and then begin to read the beginning of another (the next) word.'[105]

Reading and writing skills presumably showed a great deal of variation in terms of age, ethnicity, gender, occupational and social class, participation in the education system. When

---

103. Raquette 1909: 14, 29, 47. Written language may easily become the subject of ridicule. In cases such as this the complicated mode of expression as well as the prestige-status connected to the monopoly of types of knowledge are made fun of. (cf. Elwert 1987: 255.)
104. Scharlipp 1998: 112.

Le Coq wanted to record some items of folk poetry in Kucha, he noted that the son of the author, who had been sent to help him check and clarify the dictated texts, had a much lower level of education than his father and misread many things.[106]

Parallel use of non-verbal and verbal transmissions of knowledge can be observed in traditional forms of occupational training. Craftsmen taught their apprentices mainly through working together and through demonstrating their skills. Occupational skills were tied to traditional forms of transmitting knowledge through imitation, participation augmented by verbal explanations, but usually not by visual/graphic representation. From the second half of the nineteenth century Forsyth reports that among carpet weavers patterns did not exist on paper, but were passed from master to pupil.[107] Some occupational skills could be acquired as part of the 'domestic routine', if the household had a skilled craftsman, but typically it took the form of formal apprenticeship.[108]

3. Performers

Travellers often commented on the tremendous importance of the performing arts in Southern Xinjiang prior to the spread of Islam in the region and musical instruments and the persistent love of music and poetry are mentioned by later commentators. In Uyghur society performing artists had low social prestige. Singing, playing music, storytelling, tight rope walking and acrobatics were not recognised as specialised occupations on the same level as practitioners of more 'regular' occupations, such as tilling the land, or the trades of the blacksmith, weavers, carpenters etc.[109] One could speculate that this situation may have come about as a result of

---

105. Ibid.: 113.
106. Le Coq 1919: 51.
107. Forsyth 1875: 449.
108. Cf. Vincent 1989: 54.
109. Grenard 1898a: 161; Pantusov 1890: xi.

the conservative attitude of Muslim religious personnel to the performing arts as was common among Christians in mediaeval Europe. However, the performing arts were often the resort of mendicants, living on charity on the fringes of society who claimed to be closer to supernatural forces. Furthermore, among the neighbouring Turkic speaking Kazakh, who also professed Islam, singers and practitioners of the oral arts enjoyed higher social prestige.[110]

In his essay entitled 'Literature and Oral Art of the Uyghurs, Kazakhs and the Kirghiz' appended to his 'Pivot of Asia', Owen Lattimore draws attention to the fact that, after settling in the Tarim basin, the previously nomadic Uyghur oral traditions gradually underwent a radical change. Lattimore's classification of Uyghur oral arts, primarily based on the published materials of the Taranchi of Ili, includes proverbs, popular and fairy tales, legends, songs, and historical tales. He concludes that surviving Uyghur fairy tales are the true relics of the epic tradition characteristic of Inner Asian nomadic societies, since 'the epic character suffers with the settling of nomadic tribes'.[111] This trend was probably reinforced by the 'subsequent influence of sedentary, non-Turkic culture, and partly by the Muslim orthodoxy with its taboos against shamanistic traditions', elements of which were deeply embedded in the great Inner Asian Turkic epics.[112] This older tradition probably faded gradually in the course of the switch to a sedentary, primarily agricultural lifestyle. At the same time the value system also underwent modifications as the professional tradition-bearers were removed from their central position by a new, Islamic tradition monopolised by the clergy. However, this shift was far from complete. Singers continued to engage in oral performance and handing down traditions, but the stories they told were

---

110. Cf. Chadwick and Zhirmunsky 1969: 319-339.
111. Lattimore 1975: 248. In his comments on the German translation of selected Uyghur folk tales, Reichl also notes that the Uyghur folk tale shows traces of the epic tradition (1986: 232-3).
112. Lattimore 1975: 248.

now about the heroes of Islam, martyrs and saints, and they themselves assumed a thoroughly Islamic demeanour. Grenard, who reports the low status of these groups at the end of the nineteenth century, attributes the lack of prestige of these groups to their precarious economic existence. An additional possible explanation for the low social prestige of performers could be that most of the skills of the public performers could be 'picked up' by people who listened for long enough to the tales, who took part often enough in healing ceremonies, or who had a few years of elementary education, combined with the necessary personal charisma and self-confidence. Orally transmitted tales and songs were potentially the property of all, they could be repeated at home and handed down to the next generation. In theory at least, to acquire some of these skills one did not need to go through formal apprenticeship or even schooling, since even elementary literacy could be taught at home.

While the entertainment itself continued to be appreciated, neither the genres nor the performers were acknowledged by society as appropriate bearers of specialised knowledge. According to Grenard, 'small' *mollas* belonged to the same social group as musicians and street performers. They undertook a variety of activities such as reading and writing documents and letters for the non-literate, performing magic, casting spells and exorcising evil spirits on request and for a small fee, and occasionally delivered a public lecture in the bazaar. Professional beggars or mendicant mystics were marginal figures in society, whose stories were deeply rooted in local popular culture rather than in orthodox teachings. All these various practitioners of the verbal arts were perceived as performers.[113] Through their varied activities they were responsible for ensuring the direct and continuous exposure of large sections of the population to both the written word and to

---

113. Prov.207.II.3. Making the connection between apparently different professions was usually based on perceiving the similarities in techniques. Elsewhere, the same author, himself a *mollah*, likens the work of the *mufti* to the work of the soothsayer (Prov.207.I. 47).

forms of oral tradition. They acted as mediators between the world of respectable religious traditions and magical practices (often frowned upon by the orthodox clergy), were at home in both but belonged to neither. When their services were in demand, they most likely moved back and forth between social groups of different economic backgrounds. Their closeness to the supernatural could make them potentially dangerous, but their services were also thought to be a potential source of great benefits. In many ways, as mediators between this world and the supernatural realm, between various social groups, and between different types of traditions, they presented an anomaly, which could render their services highly valued, but them highly suspect. Regardless of which medium they used, they were essentially ambivalent figures, constantly crossing the imaginary line between orthodox and popular culture, between the realms of the 'great' and 'little' traditions.

Contradictory attitudes to various forms of the verbal arts are underlined by the different origin legends of the ġāzāl, originally a form of classic love poetry consisting of rhyming couplets, which among the Uyghur also acquired a more general meaning of love song, and therefore could constitute both a written and an oral genre. One such legend credits the well-known Islamic saint, the Prophet Xizir, with the invention of the ġāzāl. He first sang a ġāzāl disguised as a mendicant dervish (qālāndār), or a gambler (qimarwaz) and from him others learnt it. Another version insists that the ġāzāl originates from a well which was frequented by both men and women. When they approached it to fetch water, they heard a voice reciting a ġāzāl from the well and this is how people learnt how to compose ġāzāls. Yet others claim that the first ġāzāl was composed and recited by the Devil himself (šāytan) who then taught people [this art].[114] The various versions, all related by Abdulqadir (Yarkand around 1930), agree only on the supernatural/magical origins of ġāzāl, and on the fact that the knowledge of composing it was transmitted to people

---

114. Prov.464.11V.

orally.

Music (*näğmä*) and the entertainment associated with it were frowned upon by Islamic orthodoxy, and it may have been associations of the *ğäzäl* with love poetry which credited it to be the Devil's work. Music itself had controversial associations in the realm of the supernatural. According to one view, the hair of the ass of the Antichrist was made of the strings of musical instruments, which on the Day of Judgement will entice people to follow him.[115] In contrast, musicians themselves claimed Islamic origins to their skills, i.e. that music was invented by the prophet David, but the learned theologians were against it (apart from when it was played at weddings) because they associated it with the devil.[116]

Summary

Although written documentation of dispute settlement, marriage and divorce, economic transactions and dealings with the supernatural was an important element in the construction of authenticity, oral forms did not lose their force. Rather, the two modes existed alongside each other, in a complementary and often symbiotic relationship. Oral performances were closely connected to the written mode and a constantly shifting, two-way traffic between the oral and the written domains could be observed. While a high degree of prestige was attached to the written word, it could also be the subject of parody and public ridicule. Oral recitation and knowledge of sacred texts could also be attributed great value.

---

115. Jarring 1979: 16-7.
116. Prov.464.12R.

Chapter III. Education

1. Mäktäp

Direct exposure to literacy in traditional Turki society came primarily through formal education. In this chapter I shall look at forms of formal education on the primary and college level in the region and argue that formal education conformed to the patterns found elsewhere in the Islamic world. The primary or *mäktäp* education, which in principle was open to all, provided basic familiarity with the Koran, some prayers and the fundamental rules for religious and social behaviour which were closely intertwined. *Mäktäp* education may have involved simply the recital of Koran passages by pupils 'often without reading in the sense of „cracking the phonemic code". They would not necessarily be able to relate letters or clusters of letters to sounds if they encountered them in new contexts...'[117] Nevertheless, like other types of communication where the written word was offered as an available option, primary school offered basic exposure to literacy. It also promoted the prestige of the written word by connecting it to the sacred. The level of literacy skill acquired in the *mäktäp* was presumably subject to individual variation and so it is reasonable to conceive *mäktäp* education as yet another example of mixing the oral and the written modes.[118]

In pre-1949 Xinjiang as in other pre-modern societies, essential skills for living and working were transmitted with relatively little explicit use of language, either written or oral.[119] Foreigners' comments illuminate some of the strategies of early socialisation. The wife of a Swedish missionary, Sigrid Högberg, focused on issues of morality:

'Children's innocence as we understand it does not exist

---

117. Street 1984: 133.
118. Ibid.: 138.
119. Cf. Bloch 1998: 7.

here, as the children see and hear things which defile their minds long before they are able to reflect thereupon. Every word or act which implies sensuality is rewarded with an approving smile or laughter from the side of grown up people, but at the same time the youngsters are trained outwardly in a certain degree of decency, even prudishness.'[120] According to Grenard, babies were picked up as little as possible and as they grew they enjoyed considerable freedom to play in the fields and in the streets, looked after by elder siblings. Adults spoke in front of children with liberty and the latter were quickly integrated into the grown-ups' world. By the age of six or seven children were familiar with the rules of etiquette and savoir-vivre, and by ten they were accomplished businessmen. The author credited them with the ability to tell the difference between good and bad merchandise and to engage in buying and selling as required.'[121]

I have found no references to informal teaching of basic literacy skills in the domestic sphere. Although such transmission may occasionally have taken place, the institutionalised realm of the primary school was probably more important.

Grenard's positive view of domestic socialisation stood in sharp contrast to his derogatory description of methods of formal schooling, the so-called *mäktäp* education. He remarked that everybody knew the *Fatiha*, but nothing else.[122] Grenard perceived the teachers of the religious primary schools, the *mäktäp*, as possessing little knowledge. He claimed that members of the clergy and the civil administration were only marginally better educated than common people. *Mäktäp*-educated men remained semi-literate, their education comprising mainly the memorisation of Koranic verses and some very basic literacy skills, but he never heard of a single woman in Kashgaria who had even the

---

120. Högberg 1912.
121. Grenard 1898a: 131.
122. Fatiha is the first and most popular chapter of the Koran. Ibid.: 239.

rudiments of literacy.¹²³ Similarly derogatory are the words of the German scholar Martin Hartmann who commented on the sad state of both literacy and numerical skills in the region. He reported that in Kashgar anyone who was capable of reading a bit was known as a *molla* and whoever could read a three-digit number counted as a great scholar.¹²⁴ Numerical skills were scarce even among teachers. Apparently, only very few *molla*s were able to keep a proper account of time because of the relative complications of calendar computations. The beginning of the Ramadan feast in most places was therefore fixed in such a way that any person who had spotted the new moon reported it to the local religious authority, which then proclaimed this time the beginning of the feast.¹²⁵ George Hunter stated, that 'the literary problem for this people is not an easy one. A very small percentage of the Sarts can read.'¹²⁶ Negative comments about the general state of primary education and especially women's insufficient exposure to literacy were noted by the Swedish Högberg, who confirmed that few women learnt how to read.¹²⁷

Even more valuable are the insights of Nur Luke. Not only was he a native of Khotan and therefore in a position to give an insider's account but, as he wrote his work in the 1950s while in exile in India, his essay is free from the sort of self-censorship which characterises indigenous works on the subject published after 1949. As a Christian convert, however, he must have been greatly influenced by western missionaries. According to him, the pre-1949 school system by and large neglected girls. The most education girls could get was a few years in elementary school (*iptidai mäktäp*). The sole purpose of this education, which was virtually entirely of an oral nature (*zabani yani aǧzida bar tariqa örgänip*) was to teach them how to say their prayers and recite some verses from the

---

123. Grenard 1898a: 132.
124. Hartmann 1908: 47
125. Raquette 1912: 180.
126. Hunter 1920: 168.
127. Högberg 1912.

Koran. They learnt the rules of prescribed prayers (*namaz*), ritual purification (*taharat*) and fasting (*roza*). All this was completed within a year or two. He estimated that only one or two percent of girls could read the Koran, and the rest of the women remained non-literate. Therefore they remained ignorant of their own rights and men could treat them as lower than themselves. But men's position in this respect was only marginally better. Nur Luke estimated that about 97-98% of men were also uneducated (i.e. non-literate).[128] Similar opinions were expressed by Le Coq.[129] In these circumstances we must assume that the couplets referring to the '*molla*-girl', the girl who could read and write in folk materials depict the exception rather than the rule:

'The girl, who stood on the wall,
the mullah-girl with long hair,
she has in her hands inkstand and pen,
she is writing a letter, that mullah-girl.'[130]

Sources disagree as to the age when children first began school. This disagreement probably reflects variations according to region, gender, and the financial and social standing of a child's family. Forsyth reported that children started school between the ages of eight and ten, while Högberg insisted that girls began school at the age of six or seven.[131] Other sources confirm that children of both sexes went to school very young, 'the idea being that they will gradually pick up their letters.'[132] In the southern oasis centre Guma some children were apparently sent to school at the age of four or five. On the first occasion they were accompanied by a parent who would also take the teacher a bowl of food and a set of clothes. He recited a prayer and then had the gifts

---

128. Prov. 212: 21-23.
129. Grenard 1898a: 132; Le Coq 1928: 89.
130. Jarring 1948: 82, 167.
131. Forsyth 1875: 87-8; Högberg 1912;
132. Sykes and Sykes 1920: 316; Toxti 1986: 8-9.

sent to his inner quarters.¹³³

Mäktäp were erected by the residents of the neighbourhood, space often being provided by a rich patron. The classroom was near the mosque but it could also be in the teachers' house. In summer teaching was often conducted in the open air, under shady trees. Before 1930 the number of such primary schools in the city of Kashgar was approximately between seventy and eighty. The teachers known as *xälpät* or *axun* were not salaried and depended entirely on pupils' parents' donations.¹³⁴ The duration of study was not fixed. Boys could continue until they were fifteen or sixteen but girls were not allowed to go beyond the age of ten or twelve, when they were regarded as marriageable. The classes taught included the Islamic religious festivals (*Islam dini murasimliri*); Koranic verses to be recited on various occasions (*xätmä-quran qilğanda oqulidiğan ayätlar*), the Arabic script, the poetry of Allayar and Nawai in Turki and Hafiz in Persian.¹³⁵

At the end of the nineteenth century British observers gave the following account: 'Boys and girls together were seated closely packed on forms, of which the back forms the desk for the form behind it. The boys are all on one side of the room, and the girls on the other, and between is an alley, at the top of which is the seat of the teacher. The children are taught the creed and prayers from books set before them, and all gabble out their lessons with constant repetition and great volubility, and the din produced is confusing. There are several of these schools in each city, and one or more in all the market-towns of the rural settlements. The school, or *maktab*, is a low, ill-ventilated room, generally under the upper story of some private house, which is conveniently situated near a crowded thoroughfare, and some of them are amongst the shops in the bazar. Girls older than ten or twelve years don't attend, but boys are not limited to age. They are taught reading and

---

133. Jarring 1951. IV: 117-22.
134. Toxti 1986: 5.
135. Nurbaji - Goguañ 1995: 364; Toxti 1986: 8.

writing, and use as text-books the Gulistan of Sádí, and the Sikandar Nama [sic!] amongst others of less reputation. The pupils are all day scholars and pay the teacher from half a *tanga* to a *tanga* a month. Education is not compulsory, but a certain coercion is exercised on the parents to make them send their children to school.'[136]

For another insider's perspective we can refer to the work of Muhammad Ali Damolla (Kashgar,1905-10). According to him, when a person sent his child to school, his parents said: 'May the child's soul be [dedicated to] God and his body to the soil.' (*jani xudaniñ, täni topraqniñ*). The child then went to school. During wintertime children brought willow branches and they also contributed to heating expenses with half a *tañä* or thirty *pul*. Each day they started school in the morning and continued until sunset, during which time they attended three periods of instruction. When they were free to leave their teachers reminded them not to fight, to greet people they met on their way, to greet their parents upon entering their home, and to be content regardless whether they were given a small piece of bread or a whole loaf. He reminded them to say hello when entering the school and to say good-bye upon leaving. Disobedient children received their due punishment: some were put on a *bastinado*, others were hung by their hands and those who tried to run away from school had fetters put on their feet. There were other ways to restrain them and such children could then be beaten. To please God, on each Thursday children were given a meal according to their families' financial position. Schoolchildren's families had to pay a fee, which was also determined on the basis of their financial situation: rich families' children paid a sum of eight *pul* on Thursdays and four *pul* on Mondays, while the children of the poor had to pay four *pul* on Thursdays and two *pul* on Mondays. At lunch break poor children were given a piece of bread. When children started school for the first time, their parents took the teacher a tray of bread. When they finished reading the first book and started a second one, they took

---

136. Forsyth 1875: 87-8.

another tray of bread or one or two *tāṅā* cash to their teacher. This was repeated on each occasion the child began studying a new book. When a child did not come to school, other children were sent to his home to call him.[137]

Foreign observers stress the heavily oral nature of teaching, although some authors' views were formulated in more charitable terms than others. Sykes and Sykes report that Kashgar school education consisted of learning by heart a chapter of the Koran in Arabic and its Turki equivalent. Nevertheless, letters were taught and penmanship was encouraged. Furthermore, pupils were given lessons in forms of prayers and ablution.[138] In bigger schools the head teacher had to supervise the work of as many as five teachers, each one of them teaching up to fifteen children. One teacher taught the children the alphabet, another one would read the poetry of Nawai and Hafiz. The children had a long lunch break and were allowed to swim [in the summer] during the break.[139] Although we cannot be sure how many people spent even a short period of time in a *māktāp*, it seems that such education equipped them with minimal reading skills and little or no writing skills. Arabic prayers and Koranic verses were memorised without understanding them, although sometimes contents were explained in Turki. Le Coq reports that during the month of Ramadan many people in Kucha had the Koran recited without understanding the Arabic text.[140] Reports imply that *māktāp* education was not simply promoting oral modes of transmission. Rather, it was responsible for fostering the idea of the fundamental interconnectedness of oral skills

---

137. Prov.464.29R-V.
138. Sykes and Sykes 1920: 316.
139. Jarring 1951. IV: 117-22.
140. Le Coq 1928: 78. We should remember, that the acquisition of reading typically took precedence over writing in other pre-modern societies too, since the teaching and acquisition of reading is technically easier than that of writing. In England it was only in the early nineteenth century that the idea of teaching the two skills together became widespread. (Vincent 1989: 10).

and literacy.[141] The primarily religious content of the curriculum reinforced the correlation between the written word and the supernatural.

At least once a year schools gave pupils a written message, which served several purposes. Before the beginning of the Turki solar year, the *Noruz*, the teacher gave each pupil a piece of paper with some couplets written on them. They informed parents about the state of the pupil's study and wished them a good New Year. The sending of the message implied an assumption of some degree of literacy in the household. Even if parents were unable to read the message themselves, it served as a signal to encourage them to contribute to their child's education. In response, the pupils' families would give the teacher money and gifts.[142]

2. *Mādrāsā*

Male pupils who wanted to continue in further education could go to a college (*mādrāsā*). In each oasis town there were several such colleges. In the second half of the nineteenth century the city of Yarkand alone boasted fifty or sixty colleges, each of which instructed about a hundred students (*talip*).[143] At about the same time Kashgar had seventeen *mādrāsā*.[144] The number of colleges was not the only criterion for establishing a reputation as a centre of learning. At the beginning of the twentieth century Aksu was an important centre of scholarship with two *mādrāsās*, which employed several *mollas* who had spent five to ten years studying in Bukhara.[145] In 1902 Hartmann could name eleven out of the eighteen *mādrāsā* in Kashgar. He heard that in winter there were two thousand, and in summer seven hundred students studying in the Kashgar colleges. He suspected that these

---

141. Cf. Street 1984: 138.
142. Toxti 1986: 6.
143. Shaw [1871] 1984: 465.
144. Valikhanov et al. 1865: 150. These figures are the same quoted by Toxti who names all the seventeen Kashgar colleges (1986: 10-11).

figures were inflated, though some students came from as far afield as Ili and Turfan. Many of the students were not permanently studying there. They were visiting scholars who came to listen to the lectures of certain professors. In Hartmann's opinion about fifty percent of all students were idling their time away under the pretext of being students. The best known of the Kashgar professors at that time was Boha'eddin Mäxsum, whose lectures used to be attended in the winter by five hundred, and in the summer by a hundred to hundred and fifty students. In spite of his exceptional knowledge, his popularity declined after he took to opium smoking around the age of forty which caused violent outbursts. His father, Qadir axun had also been a well-known professor, the teacher of Abdulqadir, the main judge of Kashgar in 1912.[146] Towards the end of Manchu rule the number of colleges declined, with twenty-nine in Yarkand and fifteen in Kashgar.[147] The most famous Kashgar colleges at that time were the Qazançā and Xanliq *mädräsäs*, the latter alone teaching more than three hundred pupils.[148]

The denigrating tone of foreigners' reports of the state of higher education echoed their criticism of primary school practice. College education enabled students merely to read and write, to recite the Koran, and sometimes to understand its meaning. All this entitled them to call themselves *molla*.[149] Grenard reports that in the colleges there were more teachers than students, the most serious ones being those who were able to recite the Koran by heart without understanding it. Furthermore, they had some knowledge of the rudiments of Islamic law and were able to discuss some Persian books such as the Gulistan. Colleges were refectories rather than centres of learning, where the most important role was played not by the library but by the cooking pot, around which everything

---

145. Hartmann 1902: 115-6.
146. Hartmann 1908: 45-6.
147. Nurhaji - Goguañ 1995: 365-372.
148. Toxti 1986: 10-11.
149. Shaw [1871] 1984: 465.

centred. The value and reputation of a college was, in Grenard's opinion, measured according to its size and its contents.[150] Some students remained ignorant after years of studying. This was the case of a certain Sirajäddin Axun, who by 1902 had already spent seventeen years at a Kashgar college without learning anything. Such people hoped that by virtue of simply sleeping in the college throughout half their life they might acquire the 'hidden knowledge'. Some students spent as many as twenty or twenty-five years studying but remained ignorant of secular sciences.[151] Hartmann explained in a similar mode that in spite of the larger number of colleges in Yarkand, the situation there was worse than in Kashgar. The colleges were for the most part empty or they were used as shelter by the urban poor. In 1895 the total number of students was about two hundred. Out of the three professors only a certain Säfär axun was active since the other two were busy practising their other professions as *qazi* and *mufti* respectively.[152] High levels of literacy thus converged with the acquisition of specialist knowledge, especially in Islamic doctrine and law. The participation of college teachers in the religious-legal professions points to the possible shortage of sufficient literate and learned people to occupy these offices.

This Säfär axun originally came from Bukhara and at the age of seventy-eight was still teaching logic (*mantiq*) and dogma (*aqaid*). He claimed that most of the other learned men active in Eastern Turkestan at this period had been his students. At the time of Hartmann's visit he only had five or six permanent and some temporary students. In his opinion the level of college teaching and student interest did not compare favourably with that of Bukhara, where professors' lectures were accompanied by heated discussions, objections and questions put by the students. In the Yarkand *mädräsä* teaching consisted of no more than one or two hours of

---

150. Grenard 1898a: 235-6.
151. Hartmann 1908: 47; Prov. 212: 21-23.
152. Hartmann 1908: 45-9.

lectures daily.[153]

When comparing the levels of educational attainments between Western and Eastern Turkestan, the sources are contradictory. The Russian exile Nazaroff wrote that the Turkis of Eastern Turkestan were the butt of all jokes in Ferghana and Tashkent on account of their 'simplicity, ignorance and boorish manners.'[154] In contrast, Valikhanov's comparison is far more favourable for Eastern Turkestan. In his opinion, in Kokand and Bukhara the educated belonged to the spiritual/religious and commercial classes. Whoever fulfilled the formalities of religious rituals, could pepper his speech with quotations from Hafiz, Mawlana and Jami, knew some anecdotes and heroic stories, counted as knowledgeable and educated. For this kind of knowledge formal education was not even necessary, all this could be learnt from the dervishes in the bazaar. In contrast, in Eastern Turkestan every nobleman had to have some knowledge of religious dogma, of local history, of the Chinese and Manchu languages, even though their knowledge of these languages remained rather superficial. Here the clergy knew the Koran thoroughly and were acquainted with Koran commentaries and local history. They had a more correct and moderate view of things than the *mollas* of Bukhara. Literacy was more developed in the urban environment, but illiteracy remained the order of the day in the rural areas.[155]

Muhammad Ali Damolla from Kashgar (1905-10) gave an insider's description of the curriculum, according to which three branches of science were taught in the colleges. First students had to be educated in one branch of science which in most cases comprised Islamic laws. Fewer students carried on reading syntax. A few went on to study logic which 'corrected the mistakes of the intellect'.[156] Teaching normally began at about ten in the morning and continued till the midday prayer.

---

153. Ibid.: 50-1.
154. Nazaroff 1935: 48.
155. Valikhanov 1961: 345-6.
156. Prov.207.1.32.

There was some seasonal variation in the curriculum. In the wintertime students studied law and grammar, subjects considered to be difficult, while during the summer easy readings were the order of the day, such as the poetry of Jami and Rumi. The reading of elementary grammatical tracts was regarded as the basis of all further studies. Such books were lithographs prepared in Kashgar, Lahore, Istanbul and Bombay.[157] Others described traditional college curriculum as comprising Arabic and Persian language teaching, Koran explanations, traditions, Islamic history, astronomy, geography, literature, law and medicine, although the authors concede that the exact contents probably showed some variation.[158]

The colleges were charitable foundations (*waqf*) attached to shrines and sacred tombs, established by pious individuals. Like mosques, they, too, were supported by rent-free land, managed by the appointed trustees (*mutiwälli*).[159] Teachers' income was also augmented by presents provided by the families of rich students, usually at the time of religious and other festivals. Molla Abdulqadir (Yarkand, 1930) drew an egalitarian picture of college education, assuring us that college students included the sons of both urban and rural, rich and poor families. Rich students would take a good *caftan* or a sheep to the teacher, or alternatively some money (5-6 *sär*). Their contributions could also include inviting the schoolmaster to their homes in the countryside, and, as a gesture of hospitality, laying out a big feast for him in their gardens.[160] Students were normally boarders and were looked after by older students. The furniture (consisting of felt rugs, a mattress and bedding) and kitchen utensils (cups, a kettle and a tea-pot) had to be provided by his family. Poor students took some sugar as a present or could pay for their education in

---

157. Hartmann 1908: 45-9.
158. Nurhaji - Goguañ 1995: 365; Forsyth 1875:88.
159. Ibid.: 88; Prov.207.I.32.
160. Prov.464.29V-30R; Jarring 1951. IV: 123-6.

kind by serving the schoolmaster (*mudärris damolla*).¹⁶¹ In principle students with no money could get support from the income of the college's charitable foundation. The overall annual income of fifteen Kashgar colleges derived from *waqf* property amounted to 130.000 *çaräk* (13000 kg) grain. In some colleges a certain percentage of the *waqf* income was distributed among students according to their level of knowledge. The amount which they could get was usually small because the *mudärris* and the *mutiwälli* were in control of the funds and they took more for themselves. Four or five students shared a cell and they also shared their meals. After the *mudärris* had taught them a lesson, they withdrew into their cells and repeated what they had just been taught. The usual methods of learning were by way of repetition and memorisation.¹⁶² Some students studied on their own while others worked together in groups comprising five to twenty or thirty students. Occasionally group numbers could go up to seventy.¹⁶³ Some students studied throughout the six summer months without leaving the college, during which time they could receive residence allowance (*xandanliq*), presumably from the *waqf,* although this was not necessarily so.¹⁶⁴

In the beginning of the twentieth century some Kashgar colleges had students coming from Kucha, Aksu, Khotan, Yarkand. Previously students from Altä Şähär had gone to Bukhara to study.¹⁶⁵ Studying away from one's home oasis as a guest student *(misafir)* was common practice, which was explained by Mohammad Ali Damolla by the fact that students who studied in their home towns could be hindered in their

---

161. Ibid.
162. Prov. 207.I. 32; Toxti 1986: 11-2.
163. Traditional teaching was based on individual rather than collective teaching, even when children gathered in the same classroom. Collective teaching of children organised in classes according to age and level of knowledge first began in Kashgar in the 1880s (Toxti 1986: 17-8).
164. Prov.464.29V-30R
165. A similar decline of the influence of Bukhara took place among the Muslims of the Volga-Ural region in the middle of the nineteenth century. (Kemper 1998: 430, 471).

studies by the proximity of their families. What a guest student achieved in one month could not be achieved by students studying in their own hometown in the course of one year, because these latter were distracted from their studies and were inclined to play and amuse themselves.[166]

The length of study in the college was not fixed. Those who had studied for more than twenty years in a college were entitled to the title of *damolla*, i.e. learned *molla*. Studying in a college was the surest way for a Muslim to enter local bureaucracy, and the support of poor students from *waqf* funds ensured a certain degree of social mobility. However, one must assume that this was rather the exception than the rule, since poor children were typically expected from an early age to work for their families, till the land, perform corvée or earn money as day labourers. So it is not surprising that in 1922, when a new school was opened in Kashgar by Mähämmädxan, most of the one hundred pupils attending it were children of rich people.[167] In spite of the numerous schools operating in Xinjiang before the 1930s, access to education was barred by fees to most.[168]

After a man had studied in a *mädräsä*, he normally became a *molla*. After this he could also become a lower or higher ranking judge (*qazi, qazi räis*), then a *mufti*. In Yarkand when a person became a teacher in a *mädräsä*, his office could become hereditary, provided that his son also acquired the right qualifications. If he had no [male] child, then another person was appointed to his place. When a person wanted to obtain such an office, first he had to apply to the city's Chinese governor, the *ambal*. The *ambal* then could order that this person should go through an appropriate examination after which he could become appointed. There could be as many as four or five *axun* appointed to a *mädräsä*.[169] Thus, although the organisation of primary and college education remained by

---

166. Prov. 207.I.32.
167. Toxti 1986: 13
168. Mackerras 1995: 43.
169. Prov. 464. 42R.

and large a local responsibility and concern, the Chinese overlords retained a degree of control over the appointment of the educational personnel.

3. The beginnings of modern education

So far I have argued that the formal channels of transmitting knowledge in pre-1949 Xinjiang were largely under the control of the indigenous Muslim clergy, but it is important to see that this education system was not entirely stagnant. The first attempts to reform what was widely considered to have become an antiquated school system did not constitute a radical break with traditional practices. Instead they represented sometimes timid, sometimes more courageous departures from prevailing norms, building on them and expanding them. The reforms were inspired both by pragmatic as well as moral considerations. An increasing need for literacy skills in social relations was recognised, and the move away from a primarily oral culture was conceived in terms of cultural progress.

Attempts to reform traditional education dominated by religious personnel were first made in the beginning of the twentieth century. During its last years the Qing government tried to introduce compulsory education in Xinjiang, and in Kashgar Chinese and Muslim children could receive free education. Chinese language and physical drills were added to the religious curriculum but, because of Muslim opposition to state-controlled education, the whole experiment failed. These schools were closed at the beginning of the Republic, ostensibly for financial reasons, although it was most likely due to under-subscription and opposition coming from Muslims.[170]

The first successful efforts to reform the traditional Muslim education system were associated with members of the indigenous well-to-do classes. Some people had travelled abroad as merchants and were impressed by the progressive

---

170. Mackerras 1995: 43, Hunter 1920: 169.

initiatives which they had seen there. Inspiration came primarily from the examples of the Ottoman Empire and Russia rather than from China. Influences coming from Russia were most likely those of the *usul-i jadid*.[171] Initial efforts were mainly aimed at reforming teaching methods, while the contents of a fundamentally religious curriculum were not questioned. Already in the late nineteenth century there were several attempts to establish so-called *pānni* (scientific) schools in Kashgar, which, in spite of their name, did not stand in structural opposition to the traditional *māktāp*. The curriculum of these *pānni* schools was a modified version of that of the *māktāp*. It included some scientific subjects, physical education and Russian in addition to conventional subjects with a primarily Islamic orientation. Mother tongue education was also high on the agenda. These schools, however, invited the opposition of both conservative religious forces and the Chinese authorities.

In 1909 Macartney, the British representative in Kashgar, reported the following:

'For the time being, the Artushis [the people of Üstün Artush] are much under the influence of Hossain Bai Bacha, a wealthy Artushi trader, with progressive ideas of the „Young Turk" school.'[172] A more detailed account of the activities of Hossain Bay mentioned him as the sole exception to the general lethargy and conservatism prevailing in the region. He was a millionaire merchant from Artush, who had read widely and travelled extensively in Europe. In Artush he founded a charity with the aim to build schools and libraries for the education of both boys and girls. He also sponsored some young men to study abroad and set up the Artush trade company.[173] He was critical of the educational reforms initiated by the Chinese mentioned above, because the Chinese

---

171. The new, modern system devised by the Tatar Ismail Gasprinsky (1851-1914).
172. L/P & S/20. A 98, Macartney's notes from 1909. Curiously, no mention is made of Hossain Bay Baça in Toxti's detailed history of the history of education in the Kashgar area.

methods made boys disrespectful to their elders; they were losing their faith, and were more likely to turn to gambling.[174]

One of the first progressive primary schools in southern Xinjiang was established in the village of Ekisaq (in Üstün Artush), not far from Kashgar. Here progressive initiatives were continued, and in 1914 the first teachers training college was established, with Häbiboğli Ähmäd Kamal as director, who had studied in Istanbul. This establishment must have been identical with the so-called 'Young Turk' school which, according to other sources, was set up in Kashgar in 1915. Here Ähmäd Kamal is described as an Ottoman subject who introduced a curriculum based on the Ottoman model, and taught pupils to recognise the Sultan as their spiritual leader. The modern teaching methods imported from the Muslim West provoked the bitter reactions of the orthodox *mollas*. The school was officially declared unlawful (*haram*) and those who studied there were considered unbelievers *(kafir)*. Teachers of the school were imprisoned. Later the school was reopened on condition that all symbols of allegiance to the Ottoman Empire were removed and that Chinese language and military drill were added to the curriculum.[175]

Financial support to the Ekisaq school was provided by a progressive - minded merchant called Bawudun Musabay. There are some indications that, in this case at least, behind the ideological facade of conservative forces' opposition to the modernisation of education lurked economic rivalry between Musabay and another rich merchant. On one occasion, during the annual examination of the Ekisaq teachers training school, in the presence of all the important people of town (among them both progressive and conservative) some progressive students made a public proclamation: 'as long as you remain ignorant, you have no business with the motherland, with the people, with the nation! Are you passing through this world as

---

173. Skrine & Nightingale 1973: 157
174. Skrine & Nightingale 1973: 162; Forbes 1986: 18.
175. Jarring 1975: 8-9; Forbes 1986: 18; Toxti, 1986: 22-3; Mackerras 1995: 44.

an animal which only cares about filling his belly? How will you answer in front of God tomorrow? If you continue like this, you will be trailing on the ground like a snake, and will never in your life escape humiliation!' The proclamation angered the conservatives so much that eventually they filed a complaint with the Kashgar *daotai*, claiming that Bawudun Musabay had opened a new school without the permission of the Chinese authorities and that he had thereby violated local tradition. It was claimed that the common danger for both the authorities and to Islam was that students were being educated in a way comparable to military training. The students were being confused with strange subjects such as natural science and geography. This petition startled the Chinese *daotai*. Although at first Bawudun Musabay was briefly imprisoned, eventually he even succeeded in persuading the governor to open another school in Kashgar, which taught in Chinese.

While demands for education were perhaps for the first time in local history connected to nationalist slogans, modernist initiatives in the field of education did not mean a complete break with traditional religious education. On the contrary, when a modern school's expenses could not be fully met by a private sponsor, villagers' support was enrolled. Somewhat ironically, peasants' payment of the religious tax (*öşrä-zakat*) were used for supporting progressive schools.[176] Furthermore, teachers in progressive schools could simultaneously be employed in religious establishments. For example, one Tursun Äpändi who taught in the famous Ekisaq school simultaneously became a teacher at the Xanliq mädräsä in Kashgar as well as the Kashgar Teachers Training College.[177] Judging from his title, a similar background must have characterised Qasim Hajim whose school, founded in the 1910s, trained a number of students who later became schoolteachers in villages surrounding Kashgar. He was credited with recognising the need for full literacy, which included, perhaps for the first time, a simultaneous teaching of

---

176. Toxti 1986: 24-6.
177. Ibid.: 31.

reading and writing skills. His method of teaching writing was to select easy sentences from religious texts, which he then copied out and distributed to schools. During regular inspections he would then test pupils' ability both to read and write letters.[178]

In the early twentieth century some rich Turkis sent their children to be educated abroad, in the Ottoman Empire and elsewhere in the Middle East. Masud Sabri (1886-1952) who later became the first Uyghur Chairman of Xinjiang, was the son of a wealthy merchant and landlord from Ili. After studying in a Muslim college in Kulja, Masud was sent to the Ottoman Empire where he had studied at a military school before taking a medical degree from the University of Istanbul in 1914. In 1915 he returned to Xinjiang to practise medicine and at the same time he also contributed to the education reform by setting up schools. It was for these activities that he was arrested by the provincial authorities under the Chinese governor, Yang Tseng-hsin, in 1924. After his release he made an effort to place his schools under the direction of orthodox, conservative clergy to protect them from the interference of the Chinese authorities.[179]

Yang's cultural policies are illustrated by the following case. In the course of the first half of the twentieth century in the northern part of the province Soviet influence increased dramatically. For a while it was mainly spread through a library in Kulja, set up after an agreement had been concluded between Yang and the Soviets, which became the centre of progressive ideas. It advocated a modernised form of Islam, communism and women's emancipation. Such initiatives proved short-lived: Yang had the library closed down and banned Turkic language publications. Censorship badly affected education, with only the traditional Islamic schools allowed to function. Even studying foreign languages came to be regarded as suspicious.[180] Throughout the first half of the

---

178. Ibid.: 35.
179. Forbes 1986: 209.
180. Ibid.: 18-9.

twentieth century Soviet secular propaganda continued to exert its influence in the north. This was fostered by the Chinese governor, Sheng Shicai's initial Soviet-oriented policies which were to have a major impact on education. During this period in the north primary, secondary and professional schools teaching agriculture, pasture, veterinary surgery, accounting, banking etc. were run according to the Soviet model and many professionals were trained in the Soviet Union.

The 1930s saw significant progress in Kashgar's education. The most famous 'scientific' (*pänni*) schools established during this time were the schools of Norbeşi and Gülbağ. During this period increasing use was made of the *waqf* income of religious establishments for progressive educational purposes and even *mädräsä* education saw some tentative reforms. In contrast to past practice, *mädräsä* teachers now had to take a qualifying examination, and those employed were granted a regular salary. The financial and organisational management of local education was taken over by the *Uyğur mädäni aqartiş uyuşmisi* (the Association of Uyghur Cultural Enlightenment') from its predeccessor, the *Qäşqär islah madaris wä masajid häyiti* ('Association for Reforming Kashgar Mädräsäs and Mosques'). The change of name is also a symbolic indication of the gradual nationalisation of cultural development. Having recognised that teachers' knowledge itself was often inadequate, repeated efforts were made to train teachers in short courses who could then man new schools in villages and teach a reformed, partially modernised curriculum. Teacher training gained new momentum in 1934 with the establishment of a Teachers Training College in Kashgar. Students had to pass an entrance examination and the duration of study was fixed at nine months. Students could be boarders or day students, and the curriculum included mother tongue instruction, mathematics, geography, the history of China, the history of Xinjiang, ethics, religious education, physics, physical education. Between 1935-1949 3457 teachers were trained by the college. From 1934 onwards other minorities in Xinjiang too set up their equivalent of the Association for Enlightenment. In villages near Kashgar branch associations were formed. Each such branch association was overseeing four to fifteen schools, which were financed from the religious taxes *(öşrä)* of the population.[181]

The total annual income of the twenty-four branch associations belonging to Kashgar derived from religious taxes amounted to one million *çaräk* grain. Representatives of the branch associations went to the fields as soon as the harvest was over and inspected the yield. Each peasant had to give one-tenth of their harvest to the association. The amount due was written on a coupon which had to be produced upon payment. The county association's income came from the *waqf* foundations of the big shrines. In addition, the county association also received annually 10 000 livestock as part of the *zakat* payment, and each year at the Qurban Festival they also benefited from peasants' donations of the intestines and hide of sacrificial animals. The county association's annual income amounted to 1, 130 000 *çaräk* grain. This income was used to pay employees and to meet various administrative expenses, to maintain a home for the disabled, a school for orphans and for the restoration and maintenance of shrines. Most schools were maintained by the associations with the exception of the schools in Norbeşi and the Chinese school in Yeñişär which in 1934-5 were supported by the Kashgar government. The higher education college was managed by the Kashgar association. It met all the students' expenses including full board and clothes. All in all, these associations played a pioneering role in reforming local education: all over the county new schools were being built with peasants contributing labour to school construction. Smooth financial management of the associations was also taken care of: courses were organised to train accountants who could then do the job. Literacy courses for peasants were often held in individual's homes rather than in the school building. Many of those who learnt how to read and write during this time

---

181. Toxti 1986: 51-2.

became local and higher level cadres following 'Liberation' in 1949. The only secondary level specialised school in Kashgar was the Teachers College. Modern primary education took shape in this area primarily as a result of the associations' efforts. Schools were supplied with textbooks in the local language, many of which had been printed in the Soviet Union. Improving teachers' professional standards became a central concern. The annual examination system was consistently adhered to, examination committees were appointed and school inspectors regularly visited schools. The associations also built people's clubs (*xälq kulubi*) in which films were shown, theatre programmes staged and courses for musicians were organised.[182]

Although most of the above information refers to the Kashgar area in southern Xinjiang, the rest of the province presumably saw comparable developments. Mackerras reports great progress in the province's education in general between 1936 and 1942. In 1935 there were three ordinary middle schools with 425 students. By 1943 the number of such schools rose to seven with 2590 students. The number of primary schools increased from 215 in 1937 to 556 by 1942. By and large Mackerras credits Sheng with this spectacular expansion of local schools, especially primary education, which paved the way to promoting basic literacy skills. Sheng apparently encouraged ethnic diversity but made a conscious effort to eliminate the influence of the *molla*. On the other hand, Mackerras also notes the drawbacks of Sheng's education policies, which were characterised by a great deal of inflexibility and a slavish imitation of the Stalinist model. Instead of promoting ethnic unity, Sheng fostered ethnic tension, and for the most part Han Chinese were more likely to attend public schools than Muslims. Thus in 1942 6,9% of the total Uyghur population attended school, and 12 % of the total Han Chinese population.[183]

In contrast, Toxti, a local historian, attributes all educational

---

182. Ibid.: 52-57.
183. Mackerras 1995: 44-45.

development in the Kashgar region primarily to local efforts and to the excellent work of the many branches of the *Uyğur mädäni aqartiş uyuşmisi.* He views Sheng's rule as disastrous for local education. Toxti's evaluation runs as follows: Sheng had several leading teachers executed. He then proceeded to set up a rival organisation to the associations which had come about as a result of local initiative. This new organisation was known as the Kashgar County Education Office (*Qäşqär wilayätlik ma'arip idarisi*) headed by Sabit Ibrahim from Urumchi. Gradually some schools in the city and in the nearby regions, especially those which were educationally most successful, were put under the authority of the Kashgar County Education Office. These schools became known as *şänli* ('virtuous') schools, as opposed to those which remained under the associations' management, which were called *xuyli* ('bad-tempered') schools. In 1939 a Chinese named Li Yun Yang became deputy leader of the Kashgar County Education Office.[184]

In Mackerras's analysis, following Sheng's fall in 1944 the Nationalist Government left the education system in Xinjiang by and large untouched, although minor modifications were introduced. Public schools were fee paying and were therefore not accessible to all. The Republican period saw a slight increase in female education but in practice this remained extremely limited.[185] Toxti's tale is again very different. Where Mackerras implies stagnation, the local historian speaks of a dramatic decline of standards. According to the latter, following the aftermath of the uprising in 1944 in the north, many local intellectuals were imprisoned all over the province, or were placed under close observation. Primary school teachers were forcibly made join the Guomintang and spy on their colleagues. Many teachers left the profession to avoid this fate and became peasants or started to work in other sectors. Others migrated to northern Xinjiang. After Sheng fell from power, the Kashgar County Education Office was

---

184. Toxti 1986: 58-61.
185. Mackerras 1995: 53-55.

abolished and the management of schools was taken over by the County Education Divisions. The contents of school textbooks were substantially altered, with scientific explanations removed. The symbols of Sheng's rule were replaced with Guomintang symbols in the classrooms. Textbooks printed in 1937-8 in the Soviet Union were collected and burnt. Those teachers who tried to hide their books were sacked or even imprisoned. Education saw a sharp decline and both methods and the contents of the curriculum had reverted to pre-reform standards. Parents started to distrust schools and increasingly withdrew their children from formal education and once again started favouring traditional religious schools.

The years of the Nationalists' rule were characterised by increasing poverty and economic and social decline. Teachers too experienced serious economic difficulties. In 1948 the thirty-six teachers employed in the *şänli* school of Awat, which had twelve classes, received their salary in the form of bread. Each teacher received fifteen pieces of bread as a monthly salary. The teachers of *şänli* schools in principle used to be better paid than the teachers of *xuyli* schools. In practice however, the *xuyli* teachers continued to receive their salary in grain and were therefore better provided for than the teachers of the government sector. Peasants stopped paying religious taxes to the associations, which had been their main source of income. As economic standards declined, abuse of office became common. Local officials began appropriating the grains which were the associations' property. In some places officials took over the collection of religious taxes and they only handed a small proportion of these grains to the associations. The grain in the stores of the branch associations sufficed to pay teachers' salaries for five or six months only. For the rest of the year teachers were obliged to work without effective payment.[186]

---

186. Toxti 1986: 63-6. Clearly, Toxti's account is a censored publication, nevertheless we have no reason to doubt the accuracy of his account and his local knowledge. Differences in evaluating the various historical

Toxti acknowledges that Sheng set up a local education authority, but he emphasises that these became a powerful rival to successful local initiatives. He argues that the positive results attributed by Mackerras to Sheng's activities, at least in the Kashgar region, were in fact due to locally inspired initiatives. Financial support came from local merchants and from the peasantry who pooled their labour to build schools. Religious taxes paid by rural and urban populations were also utilised to support new schools. The new style, 'scientific' (*pänni*) schools did not replace traditional *mäktäp* education which was closely identified with religion. Rather, they relied on the same financial basis as the old schools and the curriculum for a long time remained a modified extension of the traditional *mäktäp* curriculum. Change was gradual and innovation largely consisted in the introduction of additional subjects rather than the abolition of religious classes. Many of the teachers were members of the religious élite and they taught in both modern and old-style schools. Teaching style and expectations changed only slowly. Initially, new-style schools continued to focus on reading, and recognition of the importance of writing skills only followed later. The cautious, gradual innovations in the education system did not prevent the persistent, parallel functioning of religious schools, which were themselves subject to minor structural changes. From all this we may tentatively conclude that religious influence over education was less dramatically weakened during the first half of the century than has been suggested.[187]

Summary

In this chapter I have given an overview of the state of traditional primary and higher education in the province. Derogatory descriptions of literacy standards by foreign and native sources emphasised teaching methods and the close

---

periods and their effects on various areas on local life can only be reduced when unlimited access to local sources becomes possible.

187. Mackerras 1995: 133.

connection with the memorising of religious texts. We have argued that in this respect, too, Eastern Turkestan was fully integrated into the Muslim world. Primary education took place in the *mäktäp* and combined teaching basic literacy and the tenets of Islam. Male students who continued in higher education proceeded to the *mädräsä* or Islamic college.

In the early twentieth century some members of the well-to-do classes, especially those who had the opportunity to visit other countries, recognised the antiquated nature of the local education system and took initiatives to reform it. Indirect evidence suggests that initial attempts at reform were inspired by the Muslim West, the Tatars of Russia and the reform initiatives of the Ottoman Empire. Literacy came to be regarded as a measure of development, but at the same time literacy and numerical skills were also increasingly needed in the economy.

These initiatives were often hindered by both the orthodox clergy and the Chinese authorities. Nevertheless, the reforms were not drastic. New style teaching continued to preserve its religious core, with new subjects being added to the old curriculum. Old and new styles of teaching continued in parallel during the first half of the twentieth century. Small reforms were also introduced in colleges, which tended to be the most resistant to change, and some religious personnel taught in both new and old style schools. The Chinese authorities, too, tried to respond to the spirit of reforms, which led to considerable tension with local initiatives. The new style of teaching paid more attention to promoting reading and writing skills, in recognition of the need for the education of skilled bureaucrats. In this period literacy skills and, by extension, education became an important arena for the struggle between traditionalists and modernisers. Literacy became increasingly identified with development and progress, and lack of it became branded. The control of education also acquired an ethnic colouring, since local initiatives to promote literacy were intimately connected to the Uyghur national 'awakening'.

Chapter IV. Literacy and oral transmission after 1949

1. Literacy and education

In this chapter it will be argued that, in spite of official promotion of literacy through repeated campaigns, oral forms of transmission have retained their dominant role among villagers in modern Xinjiang. The reason for this is that conditions for the development of 'societal literacy' have been consistently and seriously impeded.[188] Societal literacy depends upon basic social transformations, such as respect for laws, contracts and rules of association, diffusion of technical knowledge and a free 'public sphere' of debate. A strong, authoritative 'command state' prevents the emergence of open discourse and gives priority to orally transmitted orders over written laws, contracts and agreements.[189]

Like most aspects of daily life, education in Xinjiang underwent dramatic changes following 1949, when non-religious, scientific mass education became the norm. It also became the most powerful vehicle to integrate the region into the People's Republic of China. As Mackerras convincingly argues, modern education became the transmitter of Chinese patriotism and socialist ideology. Education policies followed ideological swings. During periods of tightened central control policies aimed mainly at the suppression of Islamic and ethnic consciousness and the downgrading of minority language use, but other periods have been characterised by a genuine effort to expand scientific, mass-based education among the minorities.[190]

At various levels of local authority, county and lower level officials emphasised the impressive achievements of literacy and schooling. Toxti concludes his history of Kashgar education with the following statistics: in 1949 more than 92%

---

188. Goody 1968, Street 1995, Elwert 1999.
189. Elwert 1999. On the 'command state' see Elwert forthcoming.
190. Mackerras 1995: 133-5.

of people were illiterate, in the county there were 213 primary schools with 40 000 pupils, two teachers colleges training primary school teachers with 500 pupils and one specialist school with 100 pupils. In contrast, in the mid-1980s Kashgar had two higher education colleges with 2500 students, six middle level vocational schools and an additional school for technical workers. The total number of students was 5571, 78,9% of whom were minority nationals. There were 47 *toluq* (complete) secondary schools with 12 492 pupils, 74% of whom were minority national children. The number of *toluqsiz* (incomplete, providing minimal secondary education) schools was 154, with 60 102 pupils, of whom 77,5% were minority nationals. 1267 primary schools taught 280 000 pupils. Of these 89,5% were minority nationals. In the county of Kashgar over 90% of school-age children attended school. 70% of primary school graduates went on to study in *toluqsiz* secondary schools, from which 32% of children continued to *toluq* secondary schools.[191]

When asked about local traditions, Chinese and Uyghur officials usually formulated their answers within the framework of historical evolution. In this presentation 'past' and 'present' were neatly separated by the magical date of 1949, when the province was 'peacefully liberated' by the Chinese communists. The pre-1949 situation was referred to as backward and feudal, dominated by a conservative Muslim clergy and landlords who oppressed the subject population and kept them in ignorance, while the post-'Liberation' era was described as modern and progressive, during which major economic and social advances have been made. In the mid-1990s it was admitted that during the socialist decades some mistakes had been made, but few cadres were prepared to elaborate on this. Culture was generally considered to be an important area in which development could be assessed. Local officials often mentioned proudly the achievements of

---

191. Toxti 1986: 68-9. Mackerras also reports an impressive increase of minority students in the province between 1952 and 1992 (Mackerras 1995: 137).

universal, compulsory schooling and apparent high levels of literacy among peasants, although these discussions never went much further than quoting a few statistics. No distinction was made between possession of literacy and the practical ability to use it, between the acquisitions of reading and writing skills, between the ability to write one's name and to compose a letter, between recognising numbers and being able to keep basic track of one's financial affairs.

The reform period which began in the early 1980s also brought important changes in education. In 1985 the CCP Central Committee launched a major education reform, introducing universal nine year education, consisting of six years' primary and three years' junior secondary classes. Although education has been made compulsory, as the socialist market economy was gaining momentum in the early 1990s, state control was becoming more relaxed and reportedly some poor people started to withdraw their children from education.[192]

At present a basically parallel education system prevails in Xinjiang, which, on primary and secondary levels caters separately for Han Chinese and for minority students. At these levels ethnic mixing tends to occur mainly in urban centres where some minority children attend Han Chinese schools. Although it appears to be an act of generous minority policies in full agreement with Xinjiang's autonomous status, when students proceed to further education, which requires a high level of fluency in both written and spoken Chinese, clearly minority students who have studied in Chinese schools throughout enjoy greater advantages and better career prospects. These students are fully literate in Chinese and usually also in Uyghur, but, according to my observations, their ability to read and write Uyghur fluently (functional literacy) often remains limited. Han Chinese tend not to learn minority languages, either to speak, or to write, in spite of the official policy implemented in the 1980s, which encourages all nationalities in the province, especially cadres, to learn each

---

192. Ibid.: 134-51.

other's language.[193] Exceptions to this rule are some Chinese officials who work in township party leadership, and those few Han Chinese who are permanently settled in Uyghur villages. Their children attend Uyghur village schools, and they themselves may become fluent Uyghur speakers. In the cities it is very exceptional for Han Chinese to learn Uyghur. Uyghur learn Chinese in greater numbers and Uyghur schools teach Chinese language as a compulsory subject. Nevertheless, the relative fluency of some urban Uyghur in spoken Chinese, (teachers, cadres and secondary school graduates) is usually not matched by their knowledge of the written language. Acquisition of each other's languages is therefore asymmetrical, and, given that only minority nationals educated in Chinese schools have career prospects comparable to Han Chinese, the ostensibly generous minority education policy masks discrimination rather than promotes equality.[194]

Literacy among the Uyghur in their own mother tongue is rendered more problematic by the several script changes introduced during the socialist period, the latest being a shift from the Latin script to a modified version of the Arabic alphabet in 1984. Since the problems posed by the current dual education system have been discussed elsewhere, here I shall concentrate on some forms of transmission which fall outside formal schooling and argue that traditional modes continue to persist, and in some areas remain dominant.[195]

There have been undoubted achievements in the expansion of modern education in Xinjiang. I never failed to be impressed by the number of people, young and old, who

---

193. Wei 1993: 320-322.
194. On the preferential treatment of minorities in Xinjiang see Sautman 1998: 90-94.
195. On script changes in Xinjiang see Wei 1993. On the dilemma of many Uyghur intellectuals caused by language bias in education see Rudelson 1997: 128-9. On education among the Turkic peoples of China in general see Benson 1993a and for educational policies past and present see Mackerras 1995: 39-55, 134-151. On language policy in China see Dwyer 1998.

turned up in the reading room of the town library in the oasis town where I lived in 1995. The many achievements included high figures for mass literacy and the inclusion of women in such programmes. At a meeting of a county level division of the All China Women's Association in 1995 township representatives reported on the numbers of rural women who proved to be 'good in the three studies' (*üçni öginiştä yaxşi*). The three areas were culture (*mädäniyät*), science and technology (*pen-texnika*) and politics (*siyasät*). The leader of the All China Women's Association told me that the most important aim of the organisation was to raise rural women's political and cultural standards.[196] The term *mädäniyät*, which can be translated as both culture and civilisation, is understood as a curious mixture of both local social expectations and ideological norms. Literacy was also mentioned here, although some people defined it as part of scientific-technical knowledge (*pen-texnika*). Many villagers are familiar with either the Latin or the Arabic script, thanks to a few years' schooling, but writing is rarely practised in the course of daily life. However, members of different age-groups sometimes reported complete illiteracy (*sawatsizlik*). Villagers who described themselves as illiterate generally belonged to one of the following groups: First, older people in their fifties or over, mostly but not exclusively women; Second, younger people in their early thirties whose education was either disrupted or completely neglected during their childhood, which coincided with the years of the Cultural Revolution when education was not compulsory; Third, adults who labelled themselves illiterate even though they had several years of primary school education and were able to read and write the modified Latin alphabet which was in use in Xinjiang in the 1960s and 1970s. Although courses were organised to teach this generation the Arabic script, these were

---

196. Later further conversations with Women's Association representatives in villages near Kashgar revealed that in practice in recent years the most important job of Women's Association officials in the villages ('on the ground') became the implementation of the Family Planning policy.

clearly not very effective. If written communication is required (e.g. when writing a letter to a relative or filing a petition) many people, peasants and townspeople alike, rely on the help of professional scribes. They represent another direct continuation with the past. In most towns in front of the post office there sit free-lance scribes (*xätçi*), people with some education and good calligraphy, who read, compose and write letters for a small fee.

2. The persistence of oral transmission

When asked about oral culture, township officials reported that, although folklore materials had been collected in some villages, oral culture was rapidly diminishing in this age of advanced literacy, printing, radio and television.[197] There can be no doubt that the mass production of printed books as well as the appearance of modern means of transmitting information are all associated with the socialist era and in this respect great changes have taken place. Nevertheless, the model of a traditional, backward society primarily associated with oral culture, and a post-Liberation modern one dominated by the written word does not hold. Paradoxically, the inclusion of the province into communist China in 1949 and further abrupt changes in social life since that time, more recently the accelerated modernisation taking place in the wake of the economic reforms in the early 1980s, leave plenty of room for essentially oral forms of transmission: in this respect prevailing conditions favour continuation rather than dramatic change.

---

197. Indeed, over the last twenty years a great number of volumes containing collections of Uyghur folklore, poetry, folk tales and proverbs have been published. In the township of Qoğan a primary school teacher told us that he had been collecting oral traditions. But he added that the number of knowledgeable people is decreasing. He also had a large bunch of scripts of tales, poetry etc. collected from school children, but it was hard to tell to what extent these represented examples of creative writing or more 'traditional' pieces transmitted by the older generations.

The transmission of occupational knowledge continues to show considerable resistance to switching to formal modes of transmission through schools, especially in the countryside. The years of the Great Proletarian Cultural Revolution caused major interruption not only in local education, but also in the practice and teaching of traditional crafts. Many village men, who were of school age during that time reported that they were drawn into production instead of attending school and because of the sanctions introduced against private production, many could not learn a craft either. Today these people belong to the poorest, even in generally well-to-do villages.

Since the launching of the economic reforms in the early 1980s sideline production has gained new momentum among villagers. Most peasants need additional sources of income, since their small land-holdings do not provide them with sufficient grain to feed their families and certainly with not enough cash income. After a few years in a state school boys are often apprenticed to a local master to study a craft which ensures them a degree of prestige in society and a stable source of living. In 1996 in the villages near Kashgar many peasants were engaged in sideline production as felt makers, cobblers, carpenters, wedding chest makers. Although many of these sidelines rely to a significant extent on female labour, by and large they are transmitted among men through formalised master-apprentice relationships. Some jobs, such as dairy production, sewing and the making of Uyghur embroidered caps (*doppa*) may be exclusively done by women. Apprenticing is the institutionalised form of transmission, as in the case of sewing, but informal learning from neighbours and family members dominates in the case of *doppa* making.[198] Among craftsmen the various stages of the apprenticeship ritual are meticulously observed. This involves the ceremonial taking of food to the master at the beginning, and the inviting of the master to a meal and presenting him with garments, fabric and/or money at the end of the study period. In turn the master presents the apprentice with a set of

---

198. Bellér-Hann 1998a.

tools for his trade, which is a symbolic recognition that the apprentice has fully acquired the trade skills. It also confers the blessings of the master to his pupil, without which he could not successfully practise the trade. This spiritual aspect of the transmission of specialised occupational knowledge is also present in verbal transmission of the names of the patron saint(s) of the craft, and certain formulae which craftsmen must recite at various stages of production to ensure success. These prayer formulae and codes of conduct for practitioners of the craft are usually committed to writing. The genre is known as *risalä* and a copy may also be presented by the master to the pupil at the end of his apprenticeship. Such *risalä*, which used to be entirely hand-written, circulate in the bazaars of Xinjiang nowadays in printed editions. Miniature versions may be worn by craftsmen around the neck as charms. Presumably not all craftsmen possessing a *risalä* of their profession could read, but for them too, much of the contents of the book are orally taught, and they value their copy for what it embodies.[199]

Since 1949 Muslims in Xinjiang have experienced several swings in religious policies. The worst period of religious repression was experienced during the Cultural Revolution. Although the reform period launched in the early 1980s has brought more tolerance towards formal religious practice, anything which falls outside the officially sanctioned parameters is labelled as feudal superstition which must be fought against. Religious persecution has been stepped up in the early 1990s. Cadres' participation in religious activities and the functioning of religious schools have been restricted. Conflicts caused by such repressive policies continue to be reported as secessionist attempts rather than religious persecution.[200]

As a result of this generally unfavourable climate, village mosques often have trouble in finding qualified personnel. In one village that I visited the religious functionaries (the *imam*

---

199. Habibulla, A. 1993: 313-6.
200. Mackerras 1995: 113.

and the *mäzin*) were chosen by the congregation from among the laity. These persons were regarded as suitable for the job on account of their piety, personal charisma, reliable judgement and good voice. These people were farmers with only one or two years' formal schooling. They could recite Koranic verses, prayers, and were familiar with some popular Islamic works, but they acknowledged that a great deal of their knowledge had been acquired orally. Because of the persisting restrictions on and even repression of formal education facilities for religious personnel and fear of persecution, low level *mollas* continue to be trained informally. What for men represents disruption, for female religious specialists, who have never had recourse to formal religious training, this is merely the continuation of well-established practice. The informal education of religious personnel may be done by a parent or a relative, but both men and women reported that such instruction often takes the form of master-apprentice relationship. Some books may be used, but a great deal of knowledge is transmitted orally. Such knowledge is informed, however, by popular Islamic literature. Informants stated that the curriculum closely follows Koranic teachings but admitted that other sources were also used. Some also implied that deviation from Koranic teaching in local practice was due to the fact that for a long time the Holy Book was not available in Uyghur. This was explained by a village cadre in reply to a question concerning local burial customs. In line with official policy he said that there were many practices which were mere superstitions and had nothing to do with true Islam. Then he added that such practices could appear among the Uyghur only because for a very long time they had no access to the Koran in their native tongue. This led to distortions, misinterpretation and misunderstanding of many of the Koranic teachings. Before the reforms were launched in the 1980s, particularly during the turbulent years of the Cultural Revolution, praying and most other forms of religious activities had to be carried out in secret. The lack of an

Uyghur language Koran and the stifling conditions must have enhanced the oral nature of transmission of knowledge, a method associated with the traditional *mäktäp* education before 1949.

Although in the ongoing reform period the situation in this respect is much better than before, the availability of religious books is limited. To the best of my knowledge public libraries and book shops in urban centres offer no books with religious contents, and interested members of the laity have to purchase such publications from the limited supplies of street peddlers. Some street peddlers specialise in religious publications, while others offer a selection of religious publications alongside with other, often second hand books.

Many Uyghur peasants see the government's efforts to promote compulsory education as ironic. They consider basic primary school education very important for their children, and many hope that their children (including girls) will complete the secondary level. But more than this is perceived by families with more modest means as a waste of time. Further study is considered valuable only if it leads to university education, but villagers often see this beyond their reach. Urban schools are generally considered to be better, and few villagers see a chance for their children to get through the university entrance examination. Education costs money and makes children dependent for longer. The compulsory residence registration system, which sharply distinguishes urban from rural residents, is often quoted as a means of discriminating against villagers, preventing their children from making full use of the education system. Even if a peasant family is prepared to pay for their children's education through college, several such families complained bitterly that their college-educated children, who remained rural residents, could not find employment in the city, because all the good jobs went to the children of privileged families with urban residence. Only a few people reported that they had successfully managed to change their children's residence status, usually through paying bribes. Many peasants believe that only the children of the Han Chinese and privileged Uyghur groups, namely higher level cadres children, and young people educated in Chinese schools stand a chance to get into university. Villagers complain that they were forced to attend literacy courses in the 1980s to retrain them in the Arabic script, but they have no opportunity to use their knowledge.

As in other countries with a highly centralised state, active promotion of formal education among peasants does not inhibit government offices from continuing to rely on oral means of communication with the peasants. The village loud speaker, an important tool of communal labour organisation during the collectivised period, has remained in active use. I have argued elsewhere that agricultural production and methods continue to be strictly controlled by the state.[201] Village cadres often use the communal prayer in the mosque on Fridays to disseminate agricultural or other decisions and regulations among village men after the prayer.[202] Moral campaigns initiated by the secular authority are also disseminated from the mosque, for example campaigns against excessive expenditure at weddings and funeral feasts. In its dissemination policies the state essentially promotes the methods used by traditional religious schools, and it even may make use of religious specialists to pass on such messages. On several occasions I saw a group of village *mollas* leaving the premises of the township government offices. I was told that *mollas* may sometimes be invited to join study sessions similar to those held for cadres. At such sessions they are told about new campaigns, policies and what is required from them to support these, in other words they are introduced to new codes

---

201. Bellér-Hann 1997.
202. The irony of using the religious congregation to disseminate government messages seems to be somewhat akin to the situation in pre-1949 Xinjiang, when the *mollas*, who wished to address a large audience of believers in the market place (who in pre-Communist times were often less reluctant to attend the mosque in large numbers) used the very street entertainers and performers to draw crowds whose activities they condemned. (Prov.207.II.5.)

of conduct.

Petitions to the township authorities have to be submitted in writing, and villagers may have to ask a schoolteacher relative or neighbour, or make a trip to town and engage a professional scribe to compose and write this document. But by and large the information flow is one-way, from top to bottom and it is orally transmitted. On many occasions I heard higher level officials complain of how peasants' literacy skills were insufficient for written communication. This contradicts to figures of very high literacy rates passed on to me (always orally) by township and county level cadres. Letters and documents (usually hand written) are passed around in township and village offices, but most official communication with peasants relating to the most important aspects of their livelihood, such as accounts, taxes, orders concerning production methods, and deadlines which need to be met remain oral. One office which regularly produced brief written statements distributed among the peasants was the department responsible for the highly unpopular family planning programme, but here, too, most of the dissemination was conducted orally. Local officials visit individual farmers in their home to pass on information from the authorities, to extract payment of tax, or to remind them to fulfil their outstanding duty to the state such as grain procurement. In the summer of 1996 when the county government decided to implement and enforce some new cultivation practices upon reluctant peasants, local cadres were instructed verbally at a meeting held in the fields, accompanied by a demonstration of some of the new methods. Some peasants complained that they were kept in the dark about their financial dealings with the collective and their annual tax obligations were entirely under the control of local officials. Apart from their obligation to pay grain tax to the government, notification of which is given to each farmer individually on a piece of paper, farmers never see a breakdown of the payments they are obliged to pay as tax, and as payment for services. In these conditions it is not surprising that few peasants can keep track precisely of their own accounts.[203]

The active use of reading and writing is generally perceived by peasants as closely associated with prestigious groups possessing specialised knowledge, namely cadres, teachers and religious office-holders. The prestige attached to these groups is intimately tied to ideas rooted in unequal power relations. I have argued elsewhere that, for many peasants, the active utilisation of literacy is closely tied to the idea of a higher authority. In this respect secular practice and the religious imagination reinforce each other and may even converge.[204] Peasants' moral discourse is often expressed in the concepts of sin (*guna*) and meritorious deed (*sawap*), which, according to some people, were 'written down by God himself'. As elsewhere in the Islamic world, it is commonly believed that each person has two angels sitting on his shoulders. The one on the right shoulder is responsible for keeping account of meritorious deeds, the one on the left shoulder takes notes of sins. Thus each person has a book (*däptär*) and his or her fate after death largely depends on its contents. This is called *hisaplaş* or 'accounting for'. One farmer elaborated on the parallel between religious and secular accounting explicitly: 'this is very similar to our position in the village: village leaders have our books *(däptär)* and they keep note of our duties and debts. Once a year there is an accounting for, *hisaplaş*.'

The image of an accounts book is also central to the Barat ritual, usually frowned upon by the Muslim clergy because it

---

203. In the reform period when private enterprises are blooming, small entrepreneurs tend not to keep a record of orders and expenditure. I do not exclude the possibility that regular supervision of most of my interviews prevented some people from admitting to keeping written accounts. In many cases, where the business required a simple transaction involving payment in cash, this was probably true. In many other cases the lack of functional literacy may have played a part in the lack of written records: although no written accounts were ever shown to us, many farmers gave us approximate figures concerning their brutto and netto income, after quick mental calculations. Precise figures of household production was kept by the village accountant.

204. Bellér-Hann 1997.

is regarded as non-Islamic, and by the state authorities because of its 'feudal, superstitious' character. It involves one to three nights of vigil beginning on the 15th Şā'ban during which people pray incessantly for the pardoning of their sins. According to informants this ritual serves the purpose of eliminating the sins of the past year and opening a new page in one's book (*däptär*).

The image of each person having a book kept by a superior in the hierarchy, who notes the fulfilment or dereliction of duties to higher authority, is rich in irony. Both Chinese and Islamic cultures have a long history of literacy. The authorities' insistence on predominantly oral communications with peasants reinforces peasants' conviction that literacy is useless for them, and it underscores the unequal distribution of power. More use of written means would be both a manifestation of the government's commitment to raise educational levels among farmers and a practical incentive to complete at least primary education.

3. Writing in the public sphere

While active use of literate communication between villagers and state apparatus remains limited, the written word is widely used by the authorities in the public space: on the walls of public buildings in the form of slogans to promote ideological campaigns. Some village houses, today used as private residence, preserve inscriptions from the time when the house served as the headquarters of the production brigade. The practice of using writing as a means to convey ideological message on public buildings continues, only the contents have changed: they are now promoting new campaigns, for example the planting and protection of trees and keeping the environment clean, the ideology of the unity of the country and brotherhood of the nationalities, market principles and family planning. This use of literacy is regarded as normal on the walls of township offices, but villagers object when family planning slogans in large Arabic characters appear on the outer walls of village mosques.

Other publicly displayed written messages are received with cynicism or complete disregard. In the early autumn of 1995 the central streets of one oasis centre were decorated with large slogans printed in white on red fabric, with both Chinese characters and Uyghur. I was walking into town with the Chinese characters facing me and met some acquaintances coming from the opposite side, where they could easily see and read the Uyghur language displays. In fact the displays were so large that one could avoid seeing and reading them only with great determination. My acquaintances, literate farmers returning to the nearby village, stopped me and we started chatting. I asked what the cause of the public celebrations was. They shrugged their shoulders and said, they did not know, but most likely the displays were put up in honour of the approaching Teachers' Day. They were in fact public greetings to honour the ongoing Women's Conference which had just been opened in Beijing.

In the townships of southern Xinjiang public signs and inscriptions tend to be in Uyghur only, since most villages have no or very few Han Chinese inhabitants. In urban oasis centres, however, which today all have a sizeable Han Chinese component, street signs, billboards and inscriptions on shops and public buildings are bilingual. Typically the Uyghur signs precede the Chinese characters, but the latter are displayed in much larger sizes. Book shops usually reflect the same duality, except that the Uyghur section is always smaller, there are fewer books available and the variety of Uyghur publications does not match the variety which the Chinese section has to offer. Uyghur secondary school graduates in one town complained that the number of books which have been translated from international classics was small. They knew that much more was available in Chinese, but their literacy skills in Chinese were far too limited to read in that language.[205]

---

205. These young people had learnt Chinese at school, and live in an oasis centre which has an increasing number of Han Chinese. Nevertheless, the

4. Rumour

In line with current policies to keep religious and political activists and peasants in check, publications remain subject to strict censorship.[206] Local news is often announced in the countryside and in smaller oasis towns through loudspeakers, although in the provincial capital the practice had by the mid-1990s been abandoned. Newspapers could be read in the offices which subscribed to them, and in the public library. They were not widely available in the streets, not even at the post office in town, where the newspaper stand sold magazines only. News could also reach people through television and radio, but, like newspapers, these are likely to be found in urban homes (especially in the houses of government employees) and prosperous villages. So news, especially news of local significance, tended to reach many peasants and townspeople by word of mouth, mediated by the literate local élite.

Teachers in village and small town primary schools read literary magazines with great zest. Translations of short stories from the world literature provide a small window for them on the outside world. They are interested in articles which reveal aspects of local culture. Many such articles, which concentrate on issues of Uyghur folklore and evaluate local traditions such as life cycle rituals and morality, are authored by teachers. Local reportage written in literary guise are read as valuable sources of information about social ailments such as the implementation and repercussions of new policies, excesses by local cadres, corruption, inequality and poverty. To understand these, one has to be able to read between the lines.

---

social maps of the two groups are quite sharply divided, contacts are limited to the workplace for government officials, and to a certain extent for the market place. Many young people live in a predominantly Uyghur environment.

206. There are precedents in pre-1949 Xinjiang. Hunter (1923: 205) noted that native newspapers were not allowed to be printed or circulated in the province.

This elite and all those with ready access to newspapers and other official channels of disseminating information regard the official media highly unreliable because of the prevailing strict censorship. These pressures encourage the oral circulation of news, especially those which remain altogether unreported by the official media. Such messages may enjoy a much higher level of credibility than written sources and other forms of media reporting, and different versions only add to their flavour. Naturally, the level of credibility varies according to the nature of the news, and there is also much individual variation. The local term is rumour (*miş-miş gāp*) and all social groups participate in spreading them. Topics are often politically sensitive, such as nuclear tests in the Taklamakan desert and its ecological consequences for the region, the influx of Han Chinese into the region and forms of discrimination against the Uyghur. Incidents of ethnic violence, arrests and bombings become common knowledge through rumour.[207]

These rumours may be reinforced by written publications smuggled into the region from neighbouring Kazakhstan which report news from Xinjiang. These themselves are based on rumours and on eyewitness accounts. Oral transmission is the only way of spreading news concerning violent incidents provoked by the enforced family planning programme. These often originate in cities and tell tales of violence committed against hospital staff and local officials in revenge for their involvement in forced abortions on pregnant Uyghur women. Since such stories are never covered in official publications,

---

207. During the Feast of Sacrifice in April 1996 there was an incident in a village near Kucha which resulted in the death of nine people. That the incident was not without political implications was clear. For several days it was not explicitly reported on local TV, but each news bulletin began with stern warnings and sanctions against separatist criminal activities. During these days rumours went around the city concerning the event and I heard several versions of the story, involving unpopular local cadres, abuse of power, and the suicide of the attackers when surrounded by the police. The silence of the media about the precise nature of the events was interpreted by people as a sure sign of their political relevance.

these rumours are almost always taken seriously. This high prestige of oral transmission is extended to other types of news, which may appear to be harmless or at least less politically loaded.

During my stay in Xinjiang I heard several rumours which in one way or another seemed to have wide currency, although there was a great deal of variation in how they were received and understood. An Uyghur university teacher in Urumchi told me a rumour that she knew to be a 'joke' (*çaxçaq*). According to this a few years before the President of the US had been visiting Urumchi, and he remarked that, although he had heard about the beautiful long-haired Uyghur women, in the streets of Urumchi he saw the fashionably dressed young female students with trendy short hair cuts. 'What has happened to the ornaments of Uyghur women?' he was supposed to have asked. The leaders of Xinjiang decided that this state of affairs was unacceptable and they made it a rule that Uyghur female students taking the entrance exam for university would only be admitted if they had long hair. Later on I was surprised to hear the same story repeated by some people in Kucha and in villages near Kashgar, occasionally in a more serious tone.

The frequently repeated tales about official plans to re-introduce polygamy for Muslim men came even closer to a parody of serious rumours. But often even fantastic tales may evoke some degree of credibility, as was the case with a story reminiscent of folk tales, which became important local news and concerned not a secular agency but a supernatural one. It spread rapidly in Kucha in 1996. A young school girl was reported to have met an old, badly dressed man. They passed each other in the street but did not exchange words. On the following day the same thing happened, and again they did not speak. On the third day the old man stopped her and demanded to know why she was going around without a head scarf. She is reported to have answered that he had no right to interfere with her freedom (*ärkinlik*). In response, the old man turned her head into that of a pig. My twenty-three year old female informant, a secondary school graduate, added that, although she had not witnessed this event, she had heard it from reliable sources. She also said that some people put forward a scientific explanation for the girl's appearance. According to this, not long before the girl had had bad food poisoning which (or perhaps the ensuing treatment) caused her face to be deformed. However, in the Old City many people were convinced, that the old man was none other than the Prophet Xizir, a prestigious figure in local popular culture as well as elsewhere in the Islamic world. He had had enough of the immoral 'modern' ways young Uyghur people were subscribing to. Although my informant did not start covering her head in response, her thirteen year old sister and many of her schoolmates started doing so in fear of meeting Xizir and being subjected to his punishment. My informant was reluctant to make up her mind as to which version had the greater credibility.

The above examples all concern aspects of Uyghur identity, Islamic or otherwise. They are also examples of how the high credibility of oral transmission can be exploited as a weapon of manipulation. Of course, in traditional society gossip and rumour were important means of indirect social control in small-scale communities.[208] Nowadays, in the conditions of modernisation, unauthorised subversive literature in the form of recited poems and songs is spread in the form of cassettes rather than in written form and this has political significance at the macro-level. Tapes, a popular means of circulating religious music and songs which are used for private religious gatherings and worship, are typically smuggled in from Turkey, Saudi Arabia and Pakistan. Oral transmission persists with greater force and credibility among peasants, but it also continues to exert influence among the more literate categories. Even rumours free of overt political content may serve as important means of reinforcing the self-definition of the Uyghur in emphasising religious and 'traditional' symbols,

---

208. Raquette, when relating one such true story also relates how the mean protagonist became the butt of jokes and laughter after the story had been spread in town. (Raquette 1909: 6-7, 19, 35-6.)

which in turn contribute to maintaining and strengthening local social structure. Rumours tend to be subversive and show how policies from above can become a matter of private concern.

Summary

In this chapter the role of the written and the oral was assessed within the contemporary setting of highly sensitive and potentially explosive inter-ethnic relations. As part of China's modernisation programme, modern secular schooling ensures that literacy rates have risen dramatically. However, opposing trends may be discerned. Modern education in the province is essentially a dual system. Uyghur language education fosters feelings of ethnic belonging but only Chinese-educated Uyghur youth have career prospects comparable to that of Chinese graduates. In spite of undeniable achievements in modern education, Uyghur literacy in the modern period has been hindered by several factors, for example by the several script changes, by the turbulent years of the Cultural Revolution and, more recently, by the launching of the new economic reforms in the early 1980s. A continuing impediment to the development of functional literacy, especially in the countryside, is the strong, centralised state, which insists on oral forms of communication with peasants. This 'command state' limits the prestige of the written word, because strict censorship ensures a high level of credibility for orally transmitted news and rumours, which remain just as important a means of social control as they have been in the past.

Conclusion

In this paper I have explored aspects of literate and oral communication among the Turki/Uyghur of Eastern Turkestan, Northwest China over roughly a hundred years. The period between the late nineteenth and late twentieth centuries witnessed drastic political upheavals as well as periods of accelerated modernisation. The major watershed in this respect is represented by the inclusion of the region into communist China in 1949.

The first three parts of the paper assessed the situation in the province in pre-modern times. Although this period was associated with a feudal system and illiteracy, I have argued that the written word played an important part in the life of many people, including those who could not read or write. The analysis confirms the view of Goody, Street, Finnegan and other theoreticians of literacy, who have argued that strict division of the written and the oral is artificial and does not reflect lived realities, in which various types and degrees of written and oral transmission always coexist and converge. Exposure to the written word through magical practices, civil law cases and commercial activities impinged on large sections of society, not just a handful of specialists. Over the Islamic centuries the written word acquired great significance in everyday thought, not only through the centrality of the Koran, but also because of its role in the popular imagination and local religious practices. Oral skills played an important part in traditional culture, but they did not exist in a pure, uncontaminated form.

Traditional religious schooling contributed to the spread of at least partial literacy and to the prestige of the written word among the non-literate urban and rural population. Closely connected to the development of national awaking were local initiatives, which probably played a pivotal role in the development and reforming of the traditional system. Socialist attempts to reform local education had their roots in late Imperial and especially early Republican times. The replacement of *mäktäp* literacy with a secular education system after 1949 by the Chinese socialist state represented the most dramatic departure from traditional patterns of control of knowledge. This reduced the role of Islam in education and the way opened up to secular education and to mass literacy. These developments have in theory reduced the role and importance of oral transmission.[209] Officialdom reproduces the dichotomy between oral and written, connecting the former to an era condemned as traditional, conservative and backward, and hailing increased literacy rates and mass literacy as the product of modern, secular state education.

Mass literacy programmes during the socialist period have achieved a great deal but they suffered many serious setbacks, ranging from the Cultural Revolution to politically motivated script changes. The potential of modern schooling remains seriously hindered by state policies, primarily in the countryside, where the information flow between state and peasants is still largely one sided, from top to bottom, with the state communicating many of its central messages to peasants through oral transmission.[210] Other traditional modes of transmission outside the written realm have also regained importance in the wake of the 'socialist market economy', notably through the stimulus given to traditional crafts. Topical political news reaches the urban and rural populations primarily through oral channels in the form of rumour. Because of its central role in the distribution and obtaining of

---

209. Of course, the appearance of radio, television, tape recorders and even video camcorders does effect written communication in an adverse way. However, for analytical purposes sticking to the oral - written binary opposition seems justified because these means of communication remain largely though not entirely excluded form the type of information flow discussed below. Furthermore, access to such consumer goods remains very uneven among the local population.

210. Elwert 1999.

political information, rumour that is less obviously political in nature is also taken seriously and can be a potential source for manipulation and social control. In short, past and present practice among rural and small town residents ensures that oral transmission complements the official written culture, while also continuously commenting on it and contesting it.

References

Baldick, J. 1993. *Imaginary Muslims. The Uwaysi Sufis of Central Asia.* London: I.B. Tauris.

Bellér-Hann, I. 1996 'Narratives and Values: Source Materials for the Study of Popular Culture in Xinjiang', *Inner Asia. Occasional Papers* 1(1): 89-100. (Cambridge: Mongolia and Inner Asia Studies Unit).

- 1997. 'The Peasant Condition in Xinjiang', *Journal of Peasant Studies* 25 (1): 87-112.

- 1998a. 'Work and Gender among Uighur Villagers in Southern Xinjiang', F. Aubin & J.-F. Besson (ed.) *Les Ouïgours au XXéme siècle. Cahiers d'études sur la Méditerranée orientale et le monde turco-iranien.* No. 25.. pp. 93-114.

- 1998b. 'Crafts, entrepreneurship and gendered economic relations in Southern Xinjiang in the era of „socialist commodity economy"', *Central Asian Survey* 17(4), 701-718. (Special Issue, D. Kandiyoti and R. Mandel eds.).

- forthcoming '„Making the oil fragrant". Dealings with the supernatural among the Uyghur in Xinjiang' *Asian Ethnicity.*

Bellew, H.W 1875. *Kashmir and Kashgar. A Narrative of the Journey of the Embassy to Kashgar in 1873-7,* London: Tübner & Co.

Benson, L. 1993a. 'The Turkic Peoples of China', M. Bainbridge (ed.) *The Turkic Peoples of the World,* London and New York: Kegan Paul International, pp. 53-83.

-1993b. 'A Much-Married Woman: Marriage and Divorce in Xinjiang 1850-1950' *Muslim World* 83 (3-4). pp. 227-247.

Bloch, M. 1998. *How we think they think. Anthropological approaches to cognitive memory and literacy*, Boulder: Westview Press.

Browne, E.G. 1920. *A History of Persian Literature under Tartar Dominion (A.D. 1265-1502)*. Cambridge: at the University Press.

Cable, M. & F. French 1942. *The Gobi Desert*, London: Hodder & Stoughton Limited.

Chadwick, N. and V. Zhirmunsky 1969. *Oral Epics of Central Asia*. Cambridge at the University Press.

Çızakça, M. forthcoming *A History of the Charitable Foundations, Islamic World from the Seventh Century to the Present*. Istanbul: Boğaziçi University Press.

DeWeese, D. 1996. 'The Tadhkira-i Bughra-Khan and the „Uvaysi" Sufis of Central Asia: Notes in Review of Imaginary *Muslims' Central Asiatic Journal* 40(1) 87-127.

Dwyer, A. 1998. 'The Texture of Tongues: Languages and Power in China' *Nationalism and Ethnic Politics* (Special Issue: Nationalism and Ethnoregional Identities in China) 4 (1-2). pp. 68-85.

Elwert, G. 1987. 'Die gesellschaftliche Einbettung von Schriftgebrauch' (D. Baecker, J. Markowitz u.a. hrsg.) *Theorie als Passion. Niklas Luhmann zum 60. Geburtstag.* Frankfurt am Main: Suhrkamp, 238-268.

-1999. 'Societal Literacy, Writing Culture and Development' (unpublished paper).

-forthcoming 'L'Etat commando' *Theoretical Anthropology.*

Finnegan, R. 1977. *Oral Poetry. Its nature, significance and social context*, Cambridge: Cambridge University Press.

- 1988. *Literacy and Orality.* Oxford: Blackwell.

- 1992. *Oral Traditions and the Verbal Arts. A guide to*

research practices. London and New York: Routledge.

Forbes, A.D.W. 1986. *Warlords and Muslims in Chinese Central Asia. A political history of Republican Sinkiang 1911-1949,* Cambridge: Cambridge University Press.

Forsyth, T.D. et al. 1875. *Report of a mission to Yarkund in 1873, under command of Sir T.D.Forsyth...with Historical and Geographical Information regarding the Possessions of the Ameer of Yarkund,* Calcutta: Foreign Department Press.

Franke, P. forthcoming *Begegnung mit Khidr. Quellenstudien zum Imaginären im traditionellen Islam.* Beirut/Stuttgart: Steiner. (Beiruter Texte und Studien).

Friederich, M. *Die ujghurische Literatur in Xinjiang, 1956-1966,* Wiesbaden: Harrassowitz Verlag 1997. (Turkologie und Türkeikunde 5).

Gladney, D. 1998. 'Internal colonialism and the Uyghur nationality: Chinese nationalism and ist subaltern subjects' *Cahiers d'études sur la Méditerranée orientale et le monde turco-iranien* 25: 47-63.

Goody, J. 1968. 'Restricted Literacy in northern Ghana' J. Goody (ed.) *Literacy in Traditional Societies,* Cambridge: CUP.

-1977. *The Domestication of the Savage Mind,* Cambridge: CUP.

-1982. 'Alternative Paths to Knowledge in Oral and Literate Cultures', D. Tannen (ed.) *Spoken and Written Language: Exploring Orality and Literacy.* Norwood, New Jersey: Aablex Publishing Corporation. pp. 201-15.

-1986. *The Logic of Writing and the Organisation of Society,* Cambridge: Cambridge University Press

-1987. *The interface between the written and the oral,* Cambridge: Cambridge University Press.

Grenard, F. 1898a. *Le Turkestan et le Tibet: étude*

ethongraphique et sociologique, (J.-L. Dutruil de Rhins: Mission Scientifique dans la Haute Asie 1890-1895. Deuxième partie), Paris: Ernest Leroux.

-1898b. *Histoire-Linguistique-Archéologie-Géographie,* (J.-L. Dutruil de Rhins: Mission Scientifique dans la Haute Asie 1890-1895.Troiseme partie), Paris: Ernest Leroux.

Grobe-Hagel, K. 1991. *Hinter der Grossen Mauer. Religionen und Nationalitäten in China.* Frankfurt am Main: Eichborn.

Häbibulla, A. 1993. *Uygur Etnografiyisi,* Ürümçi: Şinjañ Xälq Näşriyati.

Hartmann, M. 1902. *Der islamische Orient. Berichte und Forschungen IV. Zentralasiatisches aus Stambul.* Berlin: Wolf Peiser Verlag, pp 103-145.

-1904. 'Das Buchwesen inTurkestan und die türkischen Drucke der Sammlung Hartmann' *Mitteilungen des Seminars für Orientalische Sprachen zu Berlin,* II: Westasiatische Studien, 7. pp 69-103.

-1908. *Chinesisch-Turkestan. Geschichte, Verwaltung, Geistesleben und Wirtschaft,* Halle: Gebauer-Schwetschke Druckerei und Verlag m.b.H. (Angewandte Geographie III.Reihe 4. Band).

Haidar, Mirza Muhammad 1895. *A History of the Moghuls of Central Asia being the Tarikh-i-Rashidi of Mirza Muhammad Haidar, Doughlát,* (translated by E.D. Ross and edited by N. Elias) London: Curzon Press.

Halm, H. 1988. *Der Schia.* Darmstadt: Wissenschaftliche Buchgesellschaft.

Heath, S. B. 1983. *Ways with Words: Language, Life, and Work in Communities and Classrooms,* Cambridge: Cambridge University Press.

Högberg, S. 1912. *På obanade stigar. [On Unbeaten Tracks],* Stockholm.

Hoppe, Thomas 1998. (1995) *Die ethnischen Gruppen Xinjiangs: Kulturunterschiede und interethnische Beziehungen.* Hamburg: Institut für Asienkunde (Mitteilungen des Instituts für Asienkunde Hamburg 290). Hamburg: Institut für Asienkunde (2. Auflage).

Hultvall, J. 1981. *Mission and Change in Eastern Turkestan,* Stockholm.

Hunter, G. 1907. 'The New Province' *China's Millions* xv, N.S. pp.145-8.

-1920. 'The Chinese Moslems of Turkestan' *The Moslem World* 10. pp. 168-171.

-1923. 'Islam in Northwest China' *The Moslem World* 13. pp.203-5.

Jarring, G. 1933. *Studien zu einer osttürkischen Lautlehre,* Lund: Borelius & Leipzig: Otto Harrassowitz.

-1948. II. *Texts from Kashghar, Tashmaliq and Kucha, in Lunds Universitets Årsskrift N.F. Avd.1.* Bd 44. Nr 7.

- 1951. IV. *Ethnological and Historical texts from Guma.* in *Lunds Universitets Årsskrift N.F. Avd.1.* Bd 47.Nr.4.

-1974. 'Swedish Relations with Central Asia and Swedish Central Asian Research', *Asian Affairs* 61 (3). pp. 257-266.

-1975. *Gustav Raquette and Qasim Akhun's letters to Kamil Efendi. Ethnological and Folkloristic Materials from Southern Sinkiang,* edited and translated with explanatory notes. Lund: CWK Gleerup. (Scripta Minora Regiae Societatis Humaniorum Litterarum Lundensis 1975/76:1).

-1979. *Matters of Ethnological Interest in Swedish Missionary Reports from Southern Sinkiang,* Lund:CWK Gleerup (Scripta Minora Regiae Societatis Humaniorum Litterarum Lundensis 1979-80: 4.

-(ed.)1980. *Literary texts from Kashgar,* Lund: CWK Gleerup. (Acta Regiae Societatis Humaniorum Litterarum Lundensis.

LXXIV.)

-(ed.) 1985. *The Moen Collection of Eastern Turki (New Uighur) Proverbs and Popular Sayings*, Lund: CWK Gleerup (Scripta Minora Regiae Societatis Humaniorum Litterarum Lundensis 1984/5:1)

Katanov N. Th. 1894. 'Gadaniya u zhitelei Vostochnago Turkestana, govoryashchikh' na tatarskom' yazyk', *Zapiski Vostochnago Otdeleniya Imperatorskago Russkago Arkheologicheskago Obshchestva* 8. Pp.105-112.

Katanov - Menges 1933, 1976. *Volkskundliche Texte aus Ost-Türkistan*, Aus dem Nachlass von N. Th. Katanov. Herausgegeben von Karl Heinrich Menges. Aus den Sitzungsberichten der Preussischen Akademie der Wissenschaften Philologisch-Historische Klasse 1933 und 1936. Mit einem Vorwort zum Neudruck von Karl Heinrich Menges und einer Bibliographie der Schriften Menges' von Georg Hazai, Leipzig 1976.

Kemper, M.1998. *Sufis und Gelehrte in Tatarien und Baschkirien, 1789-1889. Der islamische Diskurs unter russischer Herrschaft.* (Islamkundliche Untersuchungen 218.) Berlin: Klaus Schwarz.

Lattimore, O. [1950] 1975. *Pivot of Asia. Sinkiang and the Inner Asian Frontiers of China and Russia*, New York: AMS Press.

Le Coq, A. von 1911. *Sprichwörter und Lieder aus der Gegend von Turfan.* (Baessler-Archiv Beiheft 1-8, 1910-17), Leipzig & Berlin.

-1916. *Volkskundliches aus Ost-Turkistan,* Berlin: Verlag von Dietrich Reimer.

-1919. *Osttürkische Gedichte und Erzählungen,* Budapest: Franklin.

-1928. *Von Land und Leuten in Ostturkistan. Berichte und Abenteuer der 4. Deutschen Turfanexpedition,* Leipzig:

dritte Auflage Verlag der J.C. Hinrichs'schen Buchhandlung.[*Buried Treasures of Chinese Turkestan. An account of the activities and adventures of the second and third German Turfan expeditions.* English translation by A. Barwell. London: George Allen & Unwin Ltd 1928].

Lipman, J. 1997. *Familiar Strangers. A History of Muslims in Northwest China.* Seattle: University of Washington Press.

L/P & S/20 A98. G. Macartney's Notes on the Road from Kashgar to Aris (Tashkent railway) via the Turgat Pass, Narin, Tokmak, Pishpek and Chimkent. 1908. London: India Office Library.

Mackerras, C. 1995. *China's Minority Cultures: Identities and Integration Since 1912,* Melbourne: St Martin Press.

-1998. 'Han-Muslim and Intra-Muslim Social Relations in Northwestern China' W. Safran (ed.) *Nationalism and Ethnoregional Identities in China.* London:Frank Cass, pp. 28-46.

Millward, J. 1998. *Beyond the Pass. Economy, Ethnicity, and Empire in Qing Central Asia, 1759- 1864,* Stanford: Stanford University Press.

Mukerji, C. & M. Schudson 1991. 'Introduction. Rethinking Popular Culture', C. Mukerji and M. Schudson (eds.) *Rethinking Popular Culture. Contemporary Perspectives in Cultural Studies,* Berkeley: University of California Press, pp. 1-61.

Schimmel, A. 1990. 'Traditionelle Frömmigkeit' Munir B. Ahmed et al. (eds.) *Islamische Kultur, zeitgenössische Strömungen, Volksfrömmigkeit* (Die Religionen der Menschheit, hrsg. Von C. Matthias Schroeder, Bd. 25. Der Islam). Stuttgart: Kohlhammer, pp. 242-266.

Nazaroff, P.S. 1935. *Moved On! From Kashgar to Kashmir,* London: George Allen & Unwin Ltd.

Nurhaji, H. and Ġ. Goguañ 1995. *Şinjañ Islam Tarixi,* Beijing:

Millätlär Näşriyati.

Ong, W. 1982. *Orality and Literacy. The Technologizing of the Word*, London and New York: Methuen.

Pantusov, N.N. 1890. *Taranchinskiya pesni*, Sanktpeterburg: Tipografiya Imperatorskoi Akademii Nauk.

-1897. *Materialy k" izucheniyu narechiya taranchei iliiskago okruga. I. Kniga o schastlivykh" i neschastlivykh" dnyakh" (taranchinskiy tekst" i russkii perevod*', Kazan: Tipo-Litografiya Imperatorskago Universiteta.

-1901. *Materialy k" izucheniyu narechiya taranchei iliiskago okruga. III. Kniga o schastlivykh" i neschastlivykh" godakh" (taranchinskii tekst" i russkii perevod")*, Kazan: Tipo-Litografiya Imperatorskago Universiteta.

-1907. *Materialy k" izucheniyu narechiya taranchei iliiskago okruga. IX. Igry taranchinskikh" detei i muzhchin"*(taranchinskii tekst", russkaya transkriptsiya I russkii perevod"). Kazan': Tipo-Litografiya Imperatorskago Universiteta

Prov. 207. I. Jarring Collection, Lund University Library.

Prov. 207. II. Jarring Collection, Lund University Library.

Prov. 212. Jarring Collection, Lund University Library.

Prov. 464. Jarring Collection, Lund University Library.

Radloff, W. 1886. *Proben der Volkslitteratur der Nördlichen Türkischen Stämme. VI. Theil: Der Dialect der Tarantschi*, St. Petersburg: Eggers & Co und J. Glasunow.

Raquette, G. 1909. *A Contribution to the Existing Knowledge of the Eastern Turkestan Dialect as it is Spoken and Written at the Present Time in the Districts of Yarkand and Kashghar*, Helsingfors: Société Finno-Ougrienne.

-1912. 'Eastern Turki Grammar. Practical and Theoretical with Vocabulary' I. *Mittelungen des Seminars für*

Orientalische Sprachen an der Königlichen Friedrich-Wilhelms-Universität zu Berlin. XV. Pp.111-183.

Raxman, Abdukerim, Räwäydulla Hämdulla, Şerip Xuştar 1996. *Uyğur Örp-Adätliri,* Ürümçi: Şinjañ Yaşlar-Ösmürlär Näşriyati.

Reichl, K. 1986. *Märchen aus Sinkiang. Überlieferungen der Turkvölker Chinas,* Köln: Diederichs.

Roberts, S. 1998. 'Negotiating locality, Islam, and national culture in a changing borderlands: the revival of the Mäshräp ritual among young Uighur men in the Ili valley', *Central Asian Survey* 17(4) 673-99.

Rudelson, J.J. 1997. *Oasis Identities. Uyghur Nationalism along China's Silk Road,* New York: Columbia University Press.

Rypka, J. 1959. *Iranische Literaturgeschichte.* Leipzig: Harrassowitz.

Sautman, B. 1998. 'Preferential Policies for Ethnic Minorities in China: The Case of Xinjiang' W. Safran (ed.) *Nationalism and Ethnoregional Identities in China.* London: Frank Cass, pp. 86-113.

Scharlipp, W. 1998. 'Two Eastern Turki texts about reading and writing', *Turkic Languages* vol. 2:1. pp. 109-125.

Schimmel, A. 1990. 'Künstlerische Ausdrucksformen des Islams' *Der Islam. III. Islamische Kultur-Zeitgenössische Strömungen-Volksfrömmigkeit* (Munir D. Ahmad et al.eds.) (Die Religionen der Menschheit Bd. 25). Stuttgart: Kohlhammer, pp.267-299.

Schoeler, G. 1985. 'Die Frage der schriftlichen oder mündlichen Überlieferung der Wissenschaften im frühen Islam' *Der Islam* 62, 201-230.

-1989. 'Weiteres zur Frage der schriftlichen oder mündlichen Überlieferung der Wissenschaften in Islam' *Der Islam* 66.

38-67.

-1996. *Charakter und Authentic der muslimischen Überlieferung über das Leben Mohammeds.* Berlin: Walter de Gruyter.

Schwarz, H.G.1992. *An Uyghur-English Dictionary*, Bellingham: Western Washington University.

Shaw, R. [1871] 1984. *Visits to High Tartary, Yarkand and Kashgar.* Hong Kong, Oxford etc: Oxford University Press. (Reprint of 1871 edition with an addition of an Introduction by P. Hopkirk).

Skrine, C.P. [1926] 1971 *Chinese Central Asia.* London: Methuen (1926); reprinted NY: Barnes & Noble, (1971).

Skrine, C.P. and P. Nightingale 1973. *Macartney at Kashgar. New Light on British, Chinese and Russian Activities in Sinkiang 1890-1918,* London: Methuen & Co. Ltd.

Street, B.V. 1984. *Literacy in theory and practice,* Cambridge: Cambridge University Press.

-(ed.) 1993. *Cross-Cultural Approaches to Literacy*, Cambridge: Cambridge University Press.

-1995. *Social literacies: critical approaches to literacy development, ethnography and education.* London: Longman.

Street, B.V. and N. Besnier 1994. 'Aspects of literacy', T. Ingold (ed.) *Companion Encyclopaedia of Anthropology* London and New York: Routledge, pp. 527-562.

Sykes, E. And P. Sykes 1920. *Through Deserts and Oases of Central Asia*, London: Macmillan and Co. Limited.

Tonkin, E. 1992. *Narrating our past. The social construction of oral history*, (Cambridge Studies in Oral and Literate Culture 22). Cambridge: Cambridge University Press.

Toxti, A. 1986. *Qäşqärniñ yeqinqi wä hazirqi zaman ma'arip tarixi,* Qäşqär: Qäşqär Uyğur Näşriyati.

Vámbéry, H. 1865. 'Ein chinesisch-tatarischer Originalbrief, übersetzt und mit Anmerkungen begleitet...' *Zeitschrift der Deutschen morgen-ländischen Gesellschaft* 19. 297-302

Valikhanof, [Ch.Ch.] Captain, M. Veniukof and other Russian travellers. 1865. *The Russians in Central Asia: their occupation of the Kirghiz steppe and the line of the Syr-Daria: their political relations with Khiva, Bokhara, and Kokan: also descriptions of Chinese Turkestan and Dzungaria.* Translated from the Russian by John and Robert Michell. London: Edward Stanford.

Valikhanov, Ch. Ch. 1961. *Sobranie Sochinenii,* Tom I. Alma-Ata: Akademii Nauk Kazakhskom SSR.

Vansina, J. 1965. *Oral Tradition,* (1961) (tr.H. M. Wright). Harmondsworth: Penguin Books.

- 1985. *Oral Tradition as History,* London and Nairobi: James Currey and Heinemann.

Vincent, D. 1989. *Literacy and Popular Culture. England 1750-1914,* Cambridge: Cambridge University Press.

Weggel, O. 1984. *Xinjiang/Sinkiang: Das zentralasiatische China. Eine Landeskunde.* Hamburg: Institut für Asienkunde.

Wei, Cuiyi 1993. 'An Historical Survey of Modern Uighur Writing since the 1950s in Xinjiang, China', *Central Asian Journal,* vol. 37. no.3-4. pp. 249-322.

Westermarck; E. 1926. *Ritual and belief in Morocco.* Vol.I. London: MacMillan.

Xutut 1937. *Xutut al-mätnäw'ä, yäni Altä şähärniñ räsmiy xät wä wäsiqäläri,* Kashgar: Svenska Missionstryckeriet.

Bei Fragen zur Produktsicherheit wenden Sie sich bitte an:
If you have any questions regarding product safety,
please contact:

Walter de Gruyter GmbH
Genthiner Straße 13
10785 Berlin
productsafety@degruyterbrill.com